POWER
of the
HOLY SPIRIT

HOLY SPIRIT POWER

REV. DR. MARCELLINE B. MUDISI - ROBINSON

AuthorHouse™ UK
1663 Liberty Drive
Bloomington, IN 47403 USA
www.authorhouse.co.uk
Phone: 0800 047 8203 (Domestic TFN)
+44 1908 723714 (International)

Because of the dynamic nature of the Internet, any web addresses or links contained in this book may have changed since publication and may no longer be valid. The views expressed in this work are solely those of the author and do not necessarily reflect the views of the publisher, and the publisher hereby disclaims any responsibility for them.

Any people depicted in stock imagery provided by Getty Images are models,
and such images are being used for illustrative purposes only.
Certain stock imagery © Getty Images.

This book is printed on acid-free paper.

Scriptures marked NIV are taken from the NEW INTERNATIONAL VERSION (NIV):
Scripture taken from THE HOLY BIBLE, NEW INTERNATIONAL VERSION ®. Copyright©
1973, 1978, 1984, 2011 by Biblica, Inc.™. Used by permission of Zondervan

Scriptures marked NKJV are taken from the NEW KING JAMES VERSION (NKJV): Scripture
taken from the NEW KING JAMES VERSION®. Copyright© 1982 by Thomas Nelson, Inc.
Used by permission. All rights reserved.

Scriptures marked RSV are taken from the REVISED STANDARD VERSION (RSV): Scripture
taken from the REVISED STANDARD VERSION, Grand Rapids: Zondervan, 1971.

Scripture quotations marked NRSV are taken from the New Revised Standard Version of the Bible,
Copyright © 1989, by the Division of Christian Education of the National Council of the Churches of
Christ in the United States of America. Used by permission. All rights reserved. Website

Scripture quotations marked NASB are taken from the New American Standard Bible®, Copyright © 1960, 1962,
1963, 1968, 1971, 1972, 1973, 1975, 1977, 1995 by The Lockman Foundation. Used by permission.

ISBN: 978-1-7283-9511-1 (sc)
ISBN: 978-1-7283-9510-4 (e)

Print information available on the last page.

Published by AuthorHouse 11/26/2019

authorHOUSE®

POWER OF THE HOLY SPIRIT

Rev. Dr. Marcelline B. Mudisi-Robinson

Rev. Dr. Marcelline B. Mudisi – Robinson
Publisher: … … …

This book is dedicated to The Lord Jesus Christ who prayed for us to God, His Father, our Father to send us The Holy Spirit.

FOREWORD

Whoso hath found a wife hath found a good thing, and hath obtained favour from Jehovah.
Proverbs 18:22 (Darby)

I was drawn by the Holy Spirit to meet a lady which led to engagement and marriage. What a privilege to have been chosen to spend the rest of my life with such a woman! We have been on a journey together through ministry training, university, ordination and receiving a honorary doctorate degree.

This book, 'Power of the Holy Spirit', is brought to you by Reverend Dr. Marcelline Mudisi-Robinson through the divine inspiration given by the Holy Spirit to help the reader grasp who the Holy Spirit is and His effect on the readers life.

The writing of this book was completed with sacrifice of many late nights, lack of food, computer eyes etc but, to the glory of God, this ninth book is worthy of being in the collection already written that glorifies God.

To my wife, I love you and so proud of you dedicating so much time to encourage others. I look forward to reading your tenth book in the making 'Reflections'

Rev. Eric Robinson PhD(h)

PREFACE

The Holy Spirit is our Helper.

Today, the Holy Spirit helps those who are not Christians to see that they are sinners so that they can repent, love and obey God. He helps Christians to become more like Jesus in conduct, faith, and attitude. The Holy Spirit has been on Earth for a long time (Genesis 1:1,2) **NIV**. He was involved in the creation of the universe; therefore, it would be safe to say that He has always been on Earth (Isaiah 40:12-15).

Why did the Holy Spirit descend from Heaven like a dove to rest on Jesus, if He was already here? (John 1:32)

The Holy Spirit is God and is not confined to the narrow concept of time and space that we have in our lives on Earth. He exists in one dimension everywhere in the universe simultaneously (Psalms 139:7,8). However, He came in a different dimension to rest upon Jesus in the form of a Dove (1). The Holy Spirit came upon Jesus to empower Him for ministry (Luke 4:14,17,18,19). Remember, Jesus is the same God who emptied Himself (1) of self (i.e., His right to all that being God entails) before being born of the Virgin Mary (Philippians 2:5 Let this mind be in you which was also in Christ Jesus: 6 Who, existing in the form of God, did not consider equality with God something to be grasped, 7 but emptied Himself, taking the form of a servant, being made in human likeness.)

Consequently, the miracles performed by Jesus were done in the power of God the Holy Spirit. (God is one, He is, Father, Son and The Holy Spirit) He manifests Himself as He sees fit or as He desires, because He is God.

Acts 10:38 NIV:

How God anointed Jesus of Nazareth with the Holy Spirit and power, and how he went around doing good and healing all who were under the power of the devil, because God was with him. When he walked the Earth; however, He had voluntarily "emptied" Himself of the right to use His power as God. He came to earth as "Son of man" empowered by the Holy Spirit to destroy the works of the devil (1 John 3:8. Hebrews 2:14). but only since Jesus Christ's ascension back to heaven, He lives inside Christians permanently.

TABLE OF CONTENTS

INTRODUCTION

Acts 1:8 **NIV**

Each Christian has God's gift of The Holy Spirit. Therefore, each Christian has spiritual "power" and should be exercising that power. Remember that Jesus said that when Holy Spirit comes, believers would have power.

John 14:12 **NIV**, says: Very truly I tell you, whoever believes in me will do the works, I have been doing, and they will do even greater things than these, because I am going to the Father.

The dramatic shift related to God's Holy Spirit that occurred on the Day of Pentecost, immediately following Christ's death and ascension to heaven. God's actions on that day were a monumental event in human history and in His great master plan of salvation. God's Holy Spirit was poured out and made available, not just to the disciples and Israel, but to nations far off and to all that God may call. Through His Spirit, God works for us and through us to bring us into His Kingdom.

1 Corinthians 12:7 **NIV**:

Now to each one the manifestation of the Spirit is given for the common good.

John 16:7 **NIV** says: But very truly I tell you, it is for your good that I am going away. Unless I go away, the Advocate will not come to you; but if I go, I will send him to you. Why did God give us the Holy Spirit? The Holy Spirit is the tangible, personified evidence that we now have total access to God through Christ. The Holy Spirit is the unbreakable seal on our salvation (Ephesians 4:30). The Holy Spirit gives us the gift of faith, resurrects our dead souls, and makes us more holy to be like Jesus himself.

The Bible is not 100% clear on this, I believe that the Holy Spirit did live in Jesus since God, The Son and The Holy Spirit are one (The Trinity), just as He lives in all Christians today. There are a number of verses that seem to point to this, but even if the Holy Spirit did not permanently dwell in Jesus while He lived on Earth, there is no question that Jesus did numerous (maybe all) things through the power of the Holy Spirit.

Several prophetic verses in Isaiah, speaking of Jesus, point to the role of the Holy Spirit in Jesus' life.

Isaiah 11:2 **NIV**: The Spirit of the LORD will rest on him- the Spirit of wisdom and of understanding, the Spirit of counsel and of might, the Spirit of the knowledge and fear of the LORD-

Isaiah 42:1 **NIV**: "Here is my servant, whom I uphold, my chosen one in whom I delight; I will put my Spirit on him, and he will bring justice to the nations.

Isaiah 61:1 **NIV**: The Spirit of the Sovereign LORD is on me, because the LORD has anointed me to proclaim good news to the poor. He has sent me to bind up the broken hearted, to proclaim freedom for the captives and release from darkness for the prisoners, (Jesus repeated this verse in Luke 4:21: **NIV** 'He began by saying to them, "Today this scripture is fulfilled in your hearing." and said it referred to Him.

Is the Holy Spirit "resting on" or "being upon" Jesus the same as "living in" Jesus? Not necessarily, but when you look up the Hebrew word for "rest" (nuwach) used in these verses, Strong's gives this as one definition, "To rest" sometimes indicates a complete envelopment and thus permeation, as in the spirit of Elijah "resting" on Elisha (2 Kin 2:15)." This certainly fits with other verses about Jesus.

At His Baptism: in Luke 3:22 **NIV**: 'and the Holy Spirit descended on him in bodily form like a dove. And a voice came from heaven: "You are my Son, whom I love; with you I am well pleased." (John 1:32-33) **NIV** Then John gave this testimony: "I saw the Spirit come down from heaven as a dove and remain on him. 33 And I myself did not know him, but the one who sent me to baptise with water told me, 'The man on whom you see the Spirit come down and remain is the one who will baptize with the Holy Spirit.'

CHAPTER 1

THE MEANING OF THE POWER OF THE HOLY SPIRIT

Acts 1:8 (NIV) says:

> But you will receive power when the Holy Spirit comes on you; and you will be my witnesses in Jerusalem, and in all Judea and Samaria, and to the ends of the earth.

What is the power Jesus was speaking of?

> For I am not ashamed of the gospel, because it is the power of God that brings salvation to everyone who believes: first to the Jew, then to the Gentile. (Romans 1:16 NIV)

It is the power to hear from God, to be convicted from sin and to receive salvation, to speak in tongues, prophesy, do signs, miracles, and wonders, and much more. In short, we can bring into evidence, into manifestation, the gift of holy spirit inside us. The gift of holy spirit, the divine nature that is sealed in each Christian, cannot be detected by the five senses. No one can see, hear, smell, taste, or touch it. However, The Holy Spirit inside all Believers, can be manifested, brought forth into evidence, in the nine ways set forth in 1 Corinthians 12:7-10:

Now to each one the manifestation of the Spirit [spirit] is given for the common good. To one there is given through the Spirit a message of wisdom, to another a message of knowledge by means of the same Spirit, to another faith by the same Spirit, to another gifts of healing by that one Spirit, to another miraculous powers, to another prophecy, to another distinguishing between spirits, to another speaking in different kinds of tongues, and to still another the interpretation of tongues.

The word "manifestation" is a good translation of the Greek *phanerosis*, which means "a manifestation; a making visible or observable." A manifestation, is detectable by the five senses. We experience manifestations all the time. Electric energy in a light bulb is manifested in the form of light and heat. A manifestation of chicken pox is a rash with small pimple-like sores. We cannot see the virus that causes the chicken pox, but we can see the manifestation of the disease.

The multipurpose "Swiss Army knife" is a good example of the difference between a gift and a manifestation. The traditional knives have red handles, and many come with two blades (big and little), two screwdrivers (flathead and crosshead), a can opener, an awl, scissors, a file, and a pair of tweezers nine manifestations!). If you receive one multipurpose knife as a gift, you can use any or all of its implements, to cut, snip, tweeze, or otherwise bring its use into manifestation. That is, the one gift has many manifestations. Similarly, the one gift God gives each believer is The Holy Spirit, which can be manifested in nine ways like a Swiss rmy knife.

The examples of the light bulb, chicken pox, and Swiss Army knife are intended to show the difference between a gift and a manifestation, but every example has limitations. The examples are meant to make the point that one gift can have many manifestations, and when a person has the gift, he has the capacity to manifest it.

The gift of holy spirit is not observable or detectable by our five senses. It' presence inside the Christian becomes known when it is manifested, made obvious, in the senses' world. 2. It may be obvious only to the one with holy spirit, such as when God gives a message of knowledge to someone and that message is known only by the one receiving it, but it is obvious in the senses' world, nonetheless.

C H A P T E R 2

MANIFESTATION OF THE HOLY SPIRIT

The Bible says that to "each one" (1 Cor. 12:7) is given the manifestation of the spirit. Each and every Christian can manifest holy spirit because each Christian has The Holy Spirit. We know there are many Christians who have never manifested the gift of The Holy Spirit in a way that they themselves recognize, and therefore they doubt that they can. We trust that this book presents convincing evidence that a Christian can manifest The Holy Spirit even if he never has done so.

What are the manifestations of The Holy Spirit? Let us return to 1 Corinthians 12:8-10:

> For to one is given through the spirit a message of wisdom; and to another, a message of knowledge because of the same spirit.

> To a different person, faith by the same spirit; and to another, a gift of healings by the one spirit;

> To another miraculous powers, to another prophecy, to another distinguishing between spirits, to another speaking in different kinds of tongues and to still another the interpretation of tongues.

4

These verses seem to indicate that each Christian gets only one manifestation, something that has confused many Christians. The phrase "to another" does not mean that each person will manifest only one of the manifestations. As we are starting to see and will learn in greater detail later, every person can manifest all nine of the manifestations. However, not everyone will manifest the spirit in the same way at any given time and place.

To make sure that things in the Church are done "decently and in order" (1 Cor. 14:40 KJV), at any given time the Lord energises different manifestations in different believers. Thus, at a Christian meeting, one person may speak in tongues and another interpret; one may prophesy and another minister healing.Believers need to step out on what the Lord is energising in them. It often happens that he is working in someone through the Holy Spirit to speak in tongues and interpret, prophesy, or pray, but the person will be too timid to step forth and manifest. The Lord will do his part, but we need to be sure we are also doing our part.

The Bible specifically says that the manifestation of holy spirit is for the "common good". Some benefit is missed or some consequence occurs when Christians do not walk with the power of the manifestations of holy spirit. Imagine the Bible with no such manifestations: no record of Moses smiting the rock, Joshua stopping the Jordan River, Samson pushing down the pagan temple, God telling Samuel to anoint Saul as king, Elijah calling down fire from heaven, or God telling Jonah to go to Nineveh.

The Bible would be much less exciting and bring much less hope and blessing if the power of God were absent from its pages. If Ananias had not walked in the power of the manifestations, he would not have had the blessing of healing Paul (Acts 9:10-18). If Peter did not walk in the power of the manifestations, he would not have had the blessing of being the first to lead Gentiles into the new birth (Acts 10:9-46). If Paul had not walked in the power of the manifestations, Eutychus would have remained dead (Acts 20:9-12). If a Christian does not speak in tongues, he misses out on the fact that to do so is a sign from God that he is saved (1 Cor.14:22). Similarly, if the manifestations are absent or misused, there are consequences. If everyone in the congregation speaks in tongues at the same time, for example, an unbeliever may get the wrong impression (1 Cor. 14: 23).

We should note that God has placed the manifestations into three groups or categories. In the verses from 1 Corinthians above, most versions read "to another" eight times. However, there are actually two different Greek words, *allos* and *heteros*, translated "to another." In Greek, *allos* was generally used to express a numerical difference and denotes "another of the same sort," while *heteros* means a qualitative difference and denotes "another of a different sort." When a list is put together and the items are said to be *allos*, they are of the same kind or nature. When they are said to be *heteros*, they are different in nature. Thus, what we see in this section is God separating the manifestations into three groups, separated by the word *heteros*, which we showed in brackets when we quoted the verses. In our translation, we used "another" when the Greek word was *allos* and "different one" when it was *heteros*.

As we study the groupings of the manifestations, it is clear that two of them are revelation (heard from God), five are related to the power of God, and two are worship oriented.

Revelation
a message of knowledge
a message of wisdom
faith

Power
gifts of healings
miracles
prophecy
discerning of spirits
speaking in tongues
interpretation of tongues

Before we examine these manifestations separately, we need to be aware that they are listed separately in the Bible and discussed separately in this book for the sake of clarity. God never intended them to be separate and distinct in the lives of the believers who experience them. He is our Father and He wants a relationship with us, and He wants us to be effective fellow-workers with Him (1 Cor. 3:9). In order to do that, we must be able to worship God (the worship group), hear from Him (the revelation group), and work for Him (the power group). In the day-to-day life of a believer who is striving to love God, live a holy life, and do God's will, the manifestations will often work seamlessly and result in great blessing for the believer and the people affected. For example, a Christian woman, Susan, may be by herself enjoying worshipping God by singing in tongues to some Christian music she is playing. Then the phone rings; it is a friend who needs prayer because many things seem to be going wrong in her life and today she is sick. Susan immediately feels the leading of the Lord to pray for specifics about her friend's life (the revelation manifestations at work) and then commands healing to take place in the name of Jesus Christ (faith and healing). By the time she gets off the phone, her friend is feeling better.

In the above scenario, Susan did not think to herself, "Now I need a message of knowledge. Now I need a message of wisdom. Now I need faith. Now I need the manifestation of gifts of healings." No, she had a relationship with God and love for her friend, and the manifestations worked together to produce the "common good" mentioned in 1 Corinthians 12:7 **NIV**.

The manifestations work together, but it is still important to understand them individually. For years scholars have discussed the manifestations of holy spirit, and there are many differing opinions. The reason for the discussion and the uncertainty is that the manifestations are not clearly defined in 1 Corinthians. There is a good reason for this. It is common in all writing that authors leave out details and descriptions that everyone knows.

Books and magazines are full of words that refer to things that in other cultures or ages may not be understood. Writers today commonly mention cars, planes, the Internet, and thousands of other things that we do not explain in detail because the readers know what they are. There are many examples of this in the Bible also.

A good example occurs in Luke, where Luke did, in his day, a good job of dating the birth of Christ by telling us it was about the time of the first census that took place while Quirinius was governor of Syria (Luke 2:2 **NIV**). No doubt everyone in Luke's day who read that said, "Ah, now I know when the birth of Christ occurred." Today, however, not much information about Quirinius has survived the centuries, and so there is controversy about the date of the birth of Christ.

Another example involves biblical animals. No doubt when Job was written, everyone knew what the "behemoth" was (Job 40:15). Today we do not know enough information for scholars to agree on what the … 'animal' is. Another example involves nations. Genesis and other books of the Bible mention the "Hittites" (Gen. 10:15 **NIV**), but that nation was lost in history so completely that until the nineteenth century, when archaeologists uncovered entire Hittite cities, some scholars even doubted their existence. Nevertheless, the Bible never describes them because the biblical readers knew exactly who they were and where they lived.

The people of Corinth and other Christians in the first century were familiar with the manifestations of holy spirit, so there was no need for Paul to explain what they were or how they worked. God's people had been manifesting holy spirit for generations (except for speaking in tongues and interpretation of tongues, with which the Corinthian Church was very familiar). God had put holy spirit upon people in the Old Testament such as Moses, Joshua, Deborah, David, Elijah, and many others, and those people could then hear knowledge or wisdom from God (thus, the message of knowledge and wisdom). They had the faith to do what God asked of them even when it seemed impossible, they did miracles, and when Jesus came on the scene, he taught his disciples to heal and cast out demons. The believers of Corinth were familiar with all these manifestations, and of course Paul, who founded the Church in Corinth on his second missionary journey (Acts 18:1-18: **NIV**), had also instructed them.

Some scholars have tried to look in Greek culture to find the meaning of the manifestations based on the definitions of the Greek words themselves (for example, "wisdom" was very important in the Greek culture). That misses the point, and for the most part has been unhelpful in discovering the nature of the manifestations and is one reason why there is so much debate about the manifestations by scholars. The manifestations were not Greek experiences or concepts, but the timeless manifestations, outward evidences, of the inward presence of holy spirit. These manifestations were not to be found in Greek culture, vocabulary, or history, but in the experiences of the men and women of God.

English culture today is somewhat similar to the Greek culture in that there has been very little accurate exposure to the power of holy spirit and very little accurate teaching on it. Therefore, we need a clear explanation of the manifestations so we can understand them. As the Greeks of old, we need to get our understanding from the Bible itself and then add to our understanding by utilising and experiencing the manifestations. We will start our study of the manifestations by giving a basic definition for each of them, and then examining them in more detail.

A message of knowledge is God or the Lord Jesus Christ providing you information, insight, and understanding about something through The Holy Spirit.

A message of wisdom is God or the Lord Jesus Christ providing to you direction, or how to apply the knowledge you have about something through The Holy Spirit.

The manifestation of faith is your having the confidence or trust that what God or the Lord Jesus Christ has revealed to you by a message of knowledge or a message of wisdom will come to pass at your command.

The manifestation of gifts of healings is you exercising your God given spiritual ability to heal by the power of God, according to what God or the Lord Jesus Christ has revealed to you by a message of knowledge or a message of wisdom through The Holy Spirit.

The manifestation of working of miracles is you exercising your God given spiritual ability to do miracles by the power of God, according to what God or the Lord Jesus Christ has revealed to you by a message of knowledge or a message of wisdom through The Holy Spirit.

Discerning of spirits is God or the Lord Jesus Christ revealing to you information about the presence or non-presence of spirits (including both holy spirit or demons), and sometimes including the identity of demons present, whether or not you may cast them out, and providing the power to do it.

Prophecy is speaking, writing, or otherwise communicating a message from God to a person or persons.

Speaking in tongues is speaking a language of men or angels that you do not understand, which is given to you by the Lord Jesus Christ through The Holy Spirit.

Interpretation of tongues is giving the sum and substance, in your own language, of what you have just spoken in tongues.

As we study these manifestations and understand what they are and how they enable each Christian to walk in spiritual power, it will be clear that every Christian can utilise all of them. The prophets of old utilised all of them but the two that God hid in Himself for the Administration of Grace speaking in tongues and the interpretation of tongues. If the prophets who had holy spirit upon them by measure utilised seven manifestations to walk powerfully before God, then surely God has not done less for us who have been filled and sealed with the gift of The Holy Spirit.

It is very important to realise that when the Bible says "manifestation of the spirit" it means exactly that these are evidences of The Holy Spirit, not natural abilities that God has given to the person. They are the presence of The Holy Spirit being made visible. We make this point because some people treat these manifestations as if they were talents that some people have, with no specific connection to the gift of The Holy Spirit they received when they were saved. It is true that God does give different people talents. Some people sing well; some people are very athletic; some are very intelligent; some people are great artists, etc. These are all God-given talents, but they are not manifestations of The Holy Spirit.

We will examine the manifestations in the order and groups that they are presented to us in the Word of God.

A Message of Knowledge and A Message of Wisdom

We will cover the two "revelation" manifestations together, because they are the first group of manifestations God mentions. They often work seamlessly together, with a single revelation from God consisting of both a message of knowledge and a message of wisdom. We call these the "revelation" manifestations because they deal with God or The Lord Jesus "revealing" something. We translate these manifestations as a "message" because the Greek word logos means an intelligible communication. The first definition of logos in Thayer's Greek Lexicon is "a word, yet not in the grammatical sense (equivalent to vocabulum, the mere name of an object), but language, vox, i.e., a word which, uttered by the living voice, embodies a conception or idea." The **NIV** uses "message," and other versions, such as the **RSV**, NRSV, and NJB, use "utterance," which would be fine as long as it is understood that it is The Lord who "utters" the message to the person and not that the person speaks a message of wisdom to someone else.

The translation "message" communicates accurately exactly what the Lord gives by revelation: a message. The message may come as an audible voice, as a picture or vision, as a physical sensation, or even as a firm realisation, an inner knowing. The King James Version says, "word of wisdom" and "word of knowledge" and so those terms are widely used, and "word" is used for "message" in Christian jargon. Nevertheless, it could be misleading to a new Bible student who might think of revelation as "words," especially because in our experience the majority of the revelation any person receives is not a "word" and not even by "words," but much more often by an impression or picture.

Since the time of Adam and Eve, it has been important for mankind to hear from God in the Old Testament He spoke through His chosen Prophets. This day and age God speaks to individuals through His word by giving them revelation through The Holy Spirit, which is knowledge, i.e., information and insight, this revelation is "a message of knowledge." He also gives wisdom, i.e., direction or what to do about a given situation, this revelation is "a message of wisdom."

CHAPTER 3

THE IMPORTANCE OF 'PROPHETS'

The prophets had the holy spirit upon them, which is why they could hear from God and then powerfully act on what He said, and why they were so revered in their culture. Is it possible for God to speak to people audibly, and not via The Holy Spirit upon or in them? If it is, true then the Bible is not very clear. When God wanted to communicate to people, He usually did so via The Holy Spirit. That is why, as we saw in Chapter 3, all through the Old Testament and the Gospels, when God wanted a person to prophesy or, like Joseph, to be a wise ruler, He put holy spirit on him. Today many Christians realise that it is possible to hear from God, it is a great blessing that today, in the Administration of Grace, each and every Christian can hear from God and the Lord Jesus Christ through reading the Holy Bible and then receiving revelation through His word, In the past God spoke to our ancestors through the prophets at many times and in various ways, 2 but in these last days he has spoken to us by his Son, whom he appointed heir of all things, and through whom also he made the universe. 3 The Son is the radiance of God's glory and the exact representation of his being, sustaining all things by his powerful word. After he had provided purification for sins, he sat down at the right hand of the Majesty in heaven. 4 So he became as much superior to the angels as the name he has inherited is superior to theirs- Hebrews1:1-4 and Hebrews 4:12 (**NIV**) says:

12 For the word of God is alive and active. Sharper than any double-edged sword, it penetrates even to dividing soul and spirit, joints and marrow; it judges the thoughts and attitudes of the heart.

When we speak of revelation from God, a message of knowledge or wisdom, we are speaking of God or the Lord Jesus giving direct revelation to the person via The Holy Spirit. Sometimes people point out that God "speaks" via other people's advice, or nature, etc. God can "speak" to us that way. Furthermore, a message of wisdom or knowledge is the Lord giving information to the believer, not the believer giving it to others. The Living Bible, for example, calls "a message of wisdom," "…the ability to give wise advice …" Many people, saved and unsaved, give wise advice. That is not a manifestation of holy spirit. The manifestation of a message of wisdom occurs when God gives a Christian a message about what to do in a given situation via the gift of The Holy Spirit.

As we saw from its definition above, the manifestation of a message of knowledge is when God or the Lord Jesus Christ gives a believer information about something. It may be only a little bit of information, but it is knowledge, nevertheless. A good example would be Joseph interpreting Pharaoh's dream (Gen. 41:25-27-**NIV**). God gave Joseph knowledge about the meaning of the dream, which was that there would be seven years of plenty, then seven years of famine. That revelation is a message of knowledge because it only gives information, the facts of the case.

When God gives someone a message of knowledge, He may give a message of wisdom so that the person will know what to do. For example, if a person has lost his car keys, all God has to do is let the person know where they are, He does not have to give a message of wisdom and say, "Go get them." The person will do that at time not even aware that he actually received a message of wisdom. Often, however, God will give a message of wisdom or He gives a message of knowledge. What if God had told Joseph about the years of plenty and the years of famine, but then never said what to do about it? The best Joseph could have done in that case would have been to pick a reasonable solution. However, God did give Joseph a message of wisdom, and Joseph told Pharaoh to store up twenty percent of the harvest during the plenteous years for the upcoming famine years (Gen. 41:33-36). When God gives a person direction, and tells him what to do, then it is "a message of wisdom."

It is important to realise and keep in mind that a message of knowledge and a message of wisdom are manifestations of The Holy Spirit and are not part of the natural human mind. They work together with the human mind, but they are separate from it. They are not superior knowledge, insight, awareness, or wisdom, which comes from the ability of the mind. Many unsaved people have great knowledge and wisdom, but these are not manifestations of holy spirit. Neither is it giving knowledge or wise advice to someone else, for many unsaved people give wise counsel to others.

A message of knowledge and a message of wisdom are God "speaking" to us to guide and help us through His word in the Bible. It is inconceivable that He would not do that for each Christian. Surely, He would not give guidance to one Christian and not to another. Every Christian can, and needs to, manifest The Holy Spirit in these two ways to live a rich and successful Christian life. No doubt most Christians have heard from God via the manifestations without even realizing it. Although there are times when God gives a message of knowledge or wisdom in such a clear and powerful way that it cannot be missed, usually God speaks in a "gentle whisper" or "a still small voice within your heart through The Holy Spirit" (1 Kings 19:12-**NIV**).

An example of the Lord giving a very clear and powerful message of knowledge and wisdom was when the Lord wanted Peter to go to the Gentiles and present the Christian message to them. The Lord gave Peter a vision and audible revelation (Acts 10:11-13 **NIV**). However, in our experience, the whisper of God can be so gentle, so quiet, that often we cannot distinguish it from our own thoughts. This is especially true in these modern times when there is probably music or television in the background, and we are so busy and distracted that we are not really paying attention to Him. That is a major reason why the definition of a message of knowledge and a message of wisdom is "God or the Lord Jesus Christ providing to you" information or direction. The Lord "provides" the information or direction, but sometimes we do not recognise it for what it is. Many times, it is only after the fact that we recognise that the "thought" we had was actually revelation from the Lord through The Holy Spirt.

Sometimes it is because of the timing of a thought or idea that we come to recognise it as revelation. Many Christians have the experience of doing something that turns out to be at "just the right time." A believer may "get the idea" to call a friend that he has not called in a long time, only to find out when he is on the phone that the timing of the call was so godly that the "idea" had to have come from the Lord. A person may "feel an urge" to stop by someone's house when he is on his way home from work, only to find that the timing of the visit was so perfect that the "urge" had to be revelation. Although sometimes these things happen by coincidence, a Christian endeavouring to walk with God and bless people will recognise them happening too frequently for that to always be the case. Often, he will be able to think back to the "idea" or the "urge" and begin to recognize that it was somehow different from a "normal thought," even though he did not recognize that at the time.

In the above examples the Lord gave the revelation at just the right time, and the effect of the believer acting on the revelation he received was that people were helped and blessed. This is a good example of how the manifestations work for the "common good" (1 Cor. 12:7 **NIV**). It is often when there is a tangible blessing in the Body of Christ that people recognise that the Lord is at work in those Christians who walk by the power of holy spirit. John 14:26 (KJV) says:

26 But the Comforter, which is the Holy Ghost, whom the Father will send in my name, he shall teach you all things, and bring all things to your remembrance, whatsoever I have said unto you.

Revelation from God or the Lord Jesus rarely comes like a flash of lightning and a crash of thunder, so very different from our own thoughts that we cannot miss it. Usually the Lord is working to help us do what we are already doing. Thus, revelation sometimes makes us aware of something that we already know, jogging our memory or "connecting the dots" for us. A good example of that is when Paul stood on trial before the Sanhedrin. Paul had been a Pharisee (Phil. 3:5 NIV) and was very aware of the tension between the Pharisees and Sadducees, who were both vying for control of the religious system in Israel. As he was brought before them, he could have been in serious trouble. They hated him, and the Romans dealt harshly with troublemakers. However, just at the right time, Paul "perceived" (Acts 23:6-**KJV**) that part of the Sanhedrin was Pharisees and part was Sadducees, and he cried out that he was a Pharisee and on trial over the issue of the resurrection of the dead. The counsel broke into pandemonium, and Paul was taken from there by the Romans who feared he would be hurt.

That Paul received revelation is quite clear from the scope of Scripture. He knew very well that part of the Sanhedrin was Pharisees and part was Sadducees, and he knew the issues over which they were divided. Therefore, it would make no sense to say that he "perceived" or "noticed" (**NRSV**) it as if he did not already know it. He knew it, but it had not occurred to him to use their division to save himself. The Lord provided the insight for Paul, and it may have saved his life.

While it is important that we do not become prideful or "spooky spiritual" and attribute all our thoughts and ideas to God, there are times when we have an "Aha" moment, or a "gut feeling," that is from God and not from our own mind. The holy spirit sealed inside of us is part of our very nature, and therefore God can communicate through it seamlessly and effortlessly to our minds. John 16: 7-9 says : But I tell you the truth, it is for your benefit that I am going away. Unless I go away, the Advocate will not come to you; but if I go, I will send Him to you. 8 And when He comes, He will convict the world in regard to sin and righteousness and judgment: 9 in regard to sin, because they do not believe in Me.

CHAPTER 4

REVELATION OF MANIFESTATIONS.

We have now discussed the revelation manifestations, a message of knowledge and a message of wisdom, and seen how they work in the lives of men and women of God. What God did for the people who had holy spirit in the Old Testament He does for Christians, because He knows we need His help and guidance to be successful in life and accomplish what He would have us accomplish. Each and every Christian should strive to live a holy life and do the work God has for Him, and then expect to receive messages of knowledge and wisdom to help and bless him.

One of the great benefits of a message of knowledge or of wisdom is that it builds our faith. It is a powerful faith-building experience to hear from heaven, and we need faith in order to accomplish that which the Lord asks us to do. Faith is the third manifestation listed in 1 Corinthians 12.

Faith
The manifestation of faith is the first manifestation that God places in the second group of manifestations, which we call the "power" manifestations. We believe that faith is the foundation of the power manifestations. "Faith" is the translation of the Greek word pistis, which means "trust," "confidence" or "assurance." We like to use the word "trust." It is important to distinguish the biblical definition of faith from today's definition that has permeated the Christian Church and society. When most people think of "faith," they think of it in terms of the modern definition: "firm belief in something for which there is no proof." When religious people have no proof for what they believe, we often hear them say, "You just have to take it by faith." It is vital to understand that "belief in something for which there is no proof" is far from the biblical definition of "faith."

The biblical definition of faith is "trust," and we trust things only after they have been proven to us. Jesus never asked anyone to believe he was the Messiah without proof. He healed the sick, raised the dead, and did miracles, such as healing the man born blind (something that had never been done in the history of the world), and he asked people to believe the miracles that he did (John 10:38 -**NIV**). Similarly, God does not ask us to believe Him without proof. He has left many evidences that He exists and that His Word is true. Thus, when God asks us to have faith, He is not asking us to believe something without proof. God proves Himself to us, and because of that we trust Him, that is, we have faith.

We must distinguish between faith as it is commonly used in the Bible and the "manifestation of faith." All of us have "faith" (trust) in a large number of things. In fact, ordinary life would be impossible without trust. A person would not sit down if he did not trust the chair would hold him. People plan their entire evening based upon faith (trust) in a recorded announcement by a total stranger as to what time the movie they want to see starts. God asks us to trust that Jesus has been raised from the dead because the Bible, history, and life give plenty of evidence for it.

In contrast to ordinary faith, the manifestation of faith is necessary to accomplish the special tasks that God, by revelation, asks us to do. For example, Jesus said that a person with faith could tell a mountain to be cast into the ocean and it would be done (Mark 11:23-**NIV**). Well, all of us have seen mountains, and we know that we do not have the human power to move them, so doing that requires the power of God. We need God to make that kind of miracle available to us by first giving us the revelation to do it. When He does, then the faith we must have in order to get the job done is "the manifestation of faith."

Moses brought water out of a rock by the manifestation of faith (Exod. 17:5 and 6 -**NIV**), Gideon defeated the Midianites by the manifestation of faith (Judg. 6:16), Elijah multiplied the oil and bread by the manifestation of faith (1 Kings 17:14-16- NIV), and the other great miracles of the Bible were done by the manifestation of faith. When it comes to miracles and gifts of healings, we need the manifestation of faith because we cannot heal the sick or do miracles by our human power. God must give us a message of knowledge and a message of wisdom, letting us know that it is His will for us to heal someone or do a miracle, and then we must have the faith to do it.

Every Christian needs to utilise the manifestation of faith. Christ said that when people received the holy spirit, they would receive power (Acts 1:8 **NIV**), but no one can operate the power of God without the faith to do so. Since every Christian needs to use the manifestation of faith to bring to pass the revelation that God gives him, every Christian has the ability to manifest faith. Thus, we see that the manifestation of faith, like a message of knowledge and a message of wisdom, is for every Christian, not just certain ones.

<u>Gifts of Healings and Working of Miracles:</u>
We cover these two manifestations together because they are similar in many ways. The "gifts [plural] of healings [plural]" is so called because God does multiple healings, and each of them is a gift, done out of His grace or mercy. Gifts of healings and working of miracles are manifestations of holy spirit because it takes a believer to do them by the power of God that he has been given. It is very important to realize that it is people, empowered by holy spirit within, who do healings and miracles. On rare occasions God heals or does a miracle without human agency, but that is not "the manifestation" of gifts of healings or miracles because the gift of holy spirit inside a Christian was not employed.

To do a healing or miracle, several manifestations come into action. First, the person needs a message of knowledge and/or a message of wisdom to know what the situation is and what to do about it. Second, he needs the manifestation of faith to bring to pass the healing or miracle. Third, he must represent Christ on earth and, via the power of God, bring to pass the miracle as God supplies the energy for it. Notice how Peter raised Tabitha:

Acts 9:40: **NIV** says 'Peter sent them all out of the room; then he got down on his knees and prayed.' Turning toward the dead woman, he said, "Tabitha, get up." She opened her eyes and seeing Peter she sat up.

Peter spoke the miracle into being. First, Peter prayed. Then, when he had revelation from the Lord to go ahead, he raised her from the dead by the power of God. Once Peter received the revelation to raise Tabitha, he performed the miracle. We believe that there would be more miracles and healings in Christendom today if Christians would step out in faith and do what the Lord tells them to do. Too often we are waiting for God to do what He has given us the spiritual power to do.

It is not our intention to demean the power of prayer in any way. Christians are commanded to pray and should do so as much as possible. However, when God or the Lord Jesus gives us the revelation to do a healing or miracle, that is not the time to pray, it is the time to step out in faith and boldly do the miracle. If the miracle or healing takes time, the one receiving the revelation must stay in faith and prayer to see it accomplished.

The book of Exodus has a great example showing that it is our choice to use the spiritual power inside us. God told Moses to take the Israelites out of Egypt. By the time they reached the sea, Pharaoh's army was close on their heels, and the people were terrified.

Exodus 14:13-16-**NIV** says:
(13) Moses answered the people, "Do not be afraid. Stand firm and you will see the deliverance the LORD will bring you today. The Egyptians you see today you will never see again.
(14) The LORD will fight for you; you need only to be still."
(15) Then the LORD said to Moses, "Why are you crying out to me? Tell the Israelites to move on.
(16) Raise your staff and stretch out your hand over the sea to divide the water so that the Israelites can go through the sea on dry ground … … … [1]

Once God gave the revelation of what to do, it was Moses' turn to act, using the power God had given him. Moses utilised the manifestation of faith and performed the miracle of splitting the sea. Had Moses not had faith to raise his staff and do the miracle, Israel would not have escaped from the Egyptians. Likewise, we Christians must recognize the power we have, and then step out and use that power.

Jesus' apostles and disciples had holy spirit upon them (John 14:17: **NIV**), which is why he could send them out to heal the sick, raise the dead, and cast out demons (Matt. 10:8; Luke 10:9: **NIV**). Furthermore, Jesus said that when people have holy spirit, they have power (Acts 1:8- NIV). It is clear that since every Christian has the gift of holy spirit, then every Christian has the power to do healings and miracles (Mark 16:17 and 18; NIV -John 14:12- NIV), just as the disciples of Christ and the prophets of old did. We need to increase our faith and step forth boldly to do what the Lord directs us to do.

The manifestations of gifts of healings and working of miracles are often interwoven. There are certainly miracles that are not healings, such as when Moses parted the sea so the Israelites could escape Egypt. Also, there are healings that are not miracles, when, although the natural power of the body to heal itself is augmented by the healing power of God, the healing is not instantaneous. However, there are many miracles of healing in the Bible, such as the instantaneous healing of Bartimaeus, who was blind (Mark 10:46-52 **NIV**). Also, casting out a demon can be a miracle (Mark 9:39 - **NIV**).

---

[1] https://www.goodsalt.com/search/red_sea_parting.html

CHAPTER 5

PROPHECY

The manifestation of prophecy is speaking, writing, or otherwise communicating a message from God to another person or persons. God or the Lord Jesus gives the Christian a message of knowledge or a message of wisdom via the holy spirit born inside him, and when he gives that message to someone else it is prophecy. The revelation that is spoken as prophecy can come in the moment, coming almost word by word as the speaker says them, something we call "inspirational prophecy." It can also come as a complete revelation given to the speaker before it is spoken as prophecy, and it can come as a combination, with some revelation coming beforehand and some coming as the prophecy is spoken. In the Old Testament, when a person had holy spirit, he or she almost always prophesied. That is why Joel said that when holy spirit was poured out on all believers, they would prophesy (Joel 2:28), and why Peter, in his teaching on the Day of Pentecost, referenced Joel.

Acts 2:17b and 18 **NIV**-
17b I, God will pour out my Spirit [spirit] on all people. Your sons and daughters will prophesy, your young men will see visions, your old men will dream dreams.

18 Even on my servants, both men and women, I will pour out my Spirit [spirit] in those days, and they will prophesy.

God says His servants will prophesy, so there should be little argument about it. The manifestation of prophecy is to strengthen, encourage and comfort people (1 Cor. 14:3 **NIV**-). It can reveal the secrets of people's hearts so that they can be closer to God (1 Cor. 14:24 and 25 **NIV**). A study of prophecy in Scripture shows that prophecy is part of the power of God, which is why God places prophecy in the "power" group of the manifestations. Some Bible teachers have placed prophecy in the "worship" group of manifestations, but prophecy is not worship, it is speaking a message from God to people. It is used in a worship service, yes, but that does not make it worship. At any given Christian service all the manifestations may come into play, depending on the needs of the people.

Many Christians do not prophesy, not because they do not have the spiritual ability. The presence of holy spirit inside a Christian gives him the ability to prophesy. If a Christian does not prophesy, either he has not been sufficiently instructed, or he does not have the faith to step out on what he has been given, or he does not want to prophesy. 1 Corinthians 14:24 **NIV**- states that the whole church can prophesy, and 1 Corinthians 14:39 (**KJV**) says "covet to prophesy."

There is a reason why each Christian should covet to prophesy. Bringing God's messages to His people is not only a tremendous privilege, it is essential for the wellbeing of the Church. A study of the Bible, especially the Old Testament, reveals how valuable the prophets were in the spiritual wholeness of the people of Israel. Prophecy is not only about speaking about the future. Not only can every Christian prophesy, as the Scripture says, but we should want to. That every believer can prophesy gives us more conclusive evidence that each believer can manifest all nine manifestations.

Discerning of Spirits

The manifestation of discerning of spirits is necessary if men and women of God are going to deal effectively with the spiritual realities of this fallen world. There are many "spirits" in this world, including angels and the gift of holy spirit. Nevertheless, because of the spiritual battle that rages around all of us, the most important aspect of discerning of spirits is dealing with the demonic forces of this world.

Ephesians 6:12 (**KJV**)
For we wrestle not against flesh and blood, but against principalities, against powers, against the rulers of the darkness of this world, against spiritual wickedness in high places.

Our Adversary, the Devil, walks about as a roaring lion, seeking people to devour (1 Pet. 5:8 - **NIV**). God has not left us helpless in that situation but has empowered us to deal with him. The manifestation of discerning of spirits is more than just recognizing them, it also involves entering into battle against them and casting them out. Recognizing demons, protecting the believers, and casting them out is all part of "discerning of spirits."

The Greek word translated "discerning" (diakrisis) has several meanings. It can mean a "distinguishing" or "differentiation." Also, it can mean to quarrel. One of the definitions in Liddell and Scott's Greek Lexicon is "decision by battle, quarrel, dispute." Thus, diakrisis can be much more than just "discerning," it has the overtones of quarrelling or fighting. Since "discerning of spirits" is a total package of recognizing "spirits" and dealing with them, God places it in the "power" group of manifestations.

The manifestation of discerning of spirits is interwoven with the other manifestations. For example, a believer manifesting discerning of spirits may be simultaneously aware of the presence of the demon, know what to do about the situation, and begin to command it to come out of the person. Receiving the information about the demon and knowing what to do is similar to and interwoven with a message of knowledge and a message of wisdom, while the casting out the demon can be in the category of a miracle (Mark 9:38 and 39), even as a healing can be a miracle (Acts 4:16).

Every Christian will encounter demons, whether he recognizes them or not. What a great blessing and comfort to know that God has equipped each of us to deal with any demon that comes against us. Ephesians 6:12 **NIV**, which says we wrestle with demonic powers, is written to every Christian.

Therefore, every Christian can manifest discerning of spirits. Referring to the Holy Spirit, Jesus affirmed in John 16:8 **NIV**- "When he comes, he will convict the world about sin, righteousness, and judgment." The Lord used the legal term "convict" in order to highlight that, even if man can point out an error, it is the Spirit that brings conviction of sin. He shows the offense, reveals the foolishness of the sin, points out the consequences, convinces of guilt, and leads the sinner to repentance. He is the church's greatest ally in its evangelising effort. Without the help and the filling of the Spirit, the evangelistic task of the church will fail.

Speaking in Tongues
Speaking in tongues is a Christian speaking a language of men or angels that he does not understand, which is given to him by the Lord Jesus Christ. It is one of the great blessings that God has given to the Christian Church, and He desires that every Christian speak in tongues.

1 Corinthians 14:5a -**NIV**- says:
I would like every one of you to speak in tongues …

The fact that God says He wants each Christian to speak in tongues should end the discussion about each person getting only one "gift" of holy spirit. If each of us can speak in tongues, then that would be the one manifestation we all would get, and there would be no need to list the other eight. This verse makes it clear that each of us can manifest holy spirit in more than one way.

The manifestations of speaking in tongues and interpretation of tongues did not exist before the Day of Pentecost. We believe that speaking in tongues is so valuable to Christians that we have dedicated Chapter 10 to it.

Interpretation of Tongues
The interpretation of tongues is interpreting, or giving the sum and substance, in one's own language, that which he has just spoken in tongues. The interpretation of tongues, like speaking in tongues itself, is given by the Lord. No one understands what he is saying in a tongue, so no one could give an interpretation of what he is saying. The interpretation comes from the Lord Jesus Christ, just as the tongue does. The manifestation of interpretation of tongues works just like speaking in tongues and prophecy do the words come from the Lord Jesus Christ to the individual via the gift of holy spirit inside him. When a person speaks in tongues in a believer's meeting, he should interpret so that the people in the meeting may be edified.

1 Corinthians 14:5 - **NIV**
I would like every one of you to speak in tongues, but I would rather have you prophesy. He who prophesies is greater than one who speaks in tongues, unless he interprets, so that the church may be edified.

The interpretation of tongues is to be done by the one who spoke in tongues, just as 1 Corinthians 14:5 - **NIV** says. Furthermore, because speaking in tongues is praise and prayer to God, the interpretation will also be to God. That is the big difference between prophecy and the interpretation of tongues. Prophecy is a message to the people (1 Cor. 14:3 **NIV**), while interpretation of tongues is to God (or the Lord Jesus Christ), but is heard by the congregation, who are then edified by it.

This section of the book has shown that each Christian has the spiritual ability to manifest all nine manifestations of holy spirit. Every Christian can talk with the Lord and receive revelation, every Christian can and should have faith and do some of the works of Jesus, every Christian should enter the spiritual battle and deal with demons, every Christian should prophesy, speak in tongues, and interpret. It is by manifesting holy spirit that Christians can walk in the power that Jesus Christ gave to the Church. We must trust God to boldly manifest holy spirit in our daily lives.

CHAPTER 6
GIFTS OR MANIFESTATIONS.

In the previous section, we spoke over and over about the "manifestations" of holy spirit. At this point we want to once again make the point that we Christians should use biblical words when we talk about the things of God. Most Christians commonly use the word "gifts" to describe what the Bible calls "manifestations" of the spirit, and this causes problems in Christianity. Why? Because words have definitive meanings, and it is through those meanings that clear communication is made possible. "Manifestation" does not mean "gift." What's the difference? A gift is individually given, and no one has a gift unless it was given to him. A manifestation is an evidence, a showing forth, of something that a person already has. There are spiritual gifts, which include holy spirit, God-given ministries such as that of an apostle or a prophet, and the gift of everlasting life (Rom. 6:23 **NIV**). But the nine manifestations are not gifts and calling them "gifts" can have a negative effect on the quality of believers' lives.

The theology of many Christians, however, reduces the difference between "gifts" and "manifestations" to a non-issue, which is one reason most commentaries make so little of it. If a person believes that he will be given at most only one of the manifestations (which is the most common teaching about the "gifts of the spirit"), then to him there is no difference between a gift and a manifestation. If the Swiss Army knife has only a knife blade, then there is not much difference between the gift of the knife and the manifestation of the blade. But if the Swiss Army knife has many blades and tools, there is a huge difference between the knife as a whole and just one blade. The difference between gift and manifestation becomes very clear and very important when one realizes that the one gift of holy spirit has many "manifestations," or evidences.

The major problem that occurs when the manifestations of holy spirit are thought to be "gifts" is that it causes many Christians to be spiritually passive. Instead of realizing that they can utilize the nine manifestations and walking in faith and speak in tongues, some believers wait on God, hoping that one day He will give them the "gift" of tongues. Other believers who would love to heal people wait for the power to heal. Such people are waiting for something they already have! They may even plead with and beg God and end up disappointed with Him for not answering their prayers. Christians need to know that they have received the power of holy spirit, and that God is waiting for them to act. They must move their mouths and speak in tongues, or use their voice to prophesy, or stretch forth their hands to heal, all with faith in the power God provided.

The theology of Bible translators is in large part responsible for people thinking that the manifestations of the spirit are gifts. Notice how often the word "gift," "gifts," or "gifted" appears in most translations of 1 Corinthians 12-14: **NIV**. Yet not one of these uses of "gift" is in the Greek text.

1 Corinthians 12:1a
Now about spiritual gifts, brothers ..."

1 Corinthians 13:2a
If I have the gift of prophecy ..."

1 Corinthians 14:1
Follow the way of love and eagerly desire spiritual gifts, especially the gift of prophecy.

1 Corinthians 14:12
So it is with you. Since you are eager to have spiritual gifts, try to excel in gifts that build up the church.

1 Corinthians 14:37a
If anybody thinks he is a prophet or spiritually gifted ..."

It is easy to see why the average Christian thinks of prophecy and the other manifestations as "spiritual gifts." It is difficult to read the Bible and come away with an accurate understanding of it when the translators have allowed their theology to distort the clear reading of the text. What is the Christian to do when he reads a version with "gifts" improperly inserted in the text? He can cross out "gifts" and make an accurate reading in the margin.

One good thing about the King James Version, American Standard Version, and New American Standard Version is that the translators italicized many words that are not in the Hebrew or Greek text, but which they added in an attempt to clarify what a verse says. In today's English writing words are sometimes italicized for emphasis. A Christian reading those versions needs to remember that the italicized words are not being emphasized, they were added to the original text.

1 Corinthians 12:1 (**KJV**)
Now concerning spiritual gifts, brethren, I would not have you ignorant.

1 Corinthians 14:1 (**KJV**)
Follow after charity, and desire spiritual gifts, but rather that ye may prophesy.

1 Corinthians 14:12 (**KJV**)
Even so ye, forasmuch as ye are zealous of spiritual gifts, seek that ye may excel to the edifying of the church.

In each of the above verses, the italics show that the word "gifts" has been added. A better translation than "spiritual gifts" is "spiritual matters" or "spiritual things," which fits the subject of 1 Corinthians 12-14, which are about spiritual matters, including "gifts" (1 Cor. 12:4), "service" (1 Cor. 12:5), "working" (energising) (1 Cor. 12:6), and "manifestations" (1 Cor. 12:7-10).

The Greek word translated "spiritual" in 1 Corinthians 12:1 and 14:1 is pneumatikos, which is an adjective, and thus needs a noun to complete the sense of the sentence. That is why the translators have supplied the noun "gifts." It is common for translators to try to get the sense of the context and supply a noun to complete the sense of pneumatikos. For example, Romans 15:27 **NIV**: says the Gentiles share in the pneumatikos of the Jews. The NIV and ESV supply "blessings," while the KJV and ASV say "things." 1 Corinthians 2:15 uses pneumatikos, and the NIV supplies "man," reading "spiritual man," while the ESV supplies "person" and reads "spiritual person," and the KJV reads "he that is spiritual." In 1 Corinthians 9:11, pneumatikos is used in the context of spiritual things that are sown into a person's life, so the NIV supplies "seed," reading "spiritual seed," while the KJV supplies "things" reading "spiritual things," and the NRSV says, spiritual "good."

The wide variety of spiritual matters being discussed in 1 Corinthians 12-14 **NIV**: dictates that "matters" or "things" be supplied to complete the sense of "spiritual" in 1 Corinthians 12:1, 14:1 **NIV**- etc. Those chapters in 1 Corinthians are speaking about spiritual matters of many kinds, not just spiritual "gifts." Adding the word "gifts" obscures what God had so clearly stated in the original text and causes people to be confused about the manifestations of holy spirit.

CHAPTER 7

BE FAMILIAR TO THE LANGUAGE OF THE BIBLE

it is important to use the word "manifestations" rather than "gifts" when referring to speaking in tongues, interpretation, prophecy, message of knowledge, etc., for a number of reasons. That is the wording that God uses, and we are always on solid ground when we use the language of the Bible. Furthermore, the word "manifestations" points to the fact that we are dealing with outward evidences of something, which in this case is the gift of holy spirit. So if speaking in tongues, etc., are manifestations of the gift, then everyone with the gift has the ability to manifest it. Are you a Christian? If so, you have holy spirit, and with it comes the power of its nine manifestations just as Christ said in Acts 1:8- **NIV**

1. There has been much scholarly discussion about the exact nature of the genitive, "of" in the phrase, "the manifestation of the spirit." The confusion is in large part due to the fact that most theologians think the "Spirit" is God. The spirit in this verse is the gift of God, holy spirit, and the genitive is the genitive of origin. The gift of holy spirit is the source of the manifestations. Another parallel phrase occurs in 2 Corinthians 4:2, which has "the manifestation of the truth" (**KJV**, which has the articles accurately placed). This also is a genitive of origin. One cannot see the "truth" in the apostles' minds, but it is there, and it is the origin of their behaviour, which can be seen by everyone. The gift of holy spirit and "truth" are invisible in a person, but they produce manifestations that can be clearly seen in the sense's world.

2. It is "because of the same spirit," the gift of holy spirit inside him, that a person can receive revelation.

3. The use of "to one … to another …" has caused great confusion in the Church.

4. Knowledge is information about a situation, while wisdom is what to do about the situation.

5. How to Hear from God for example "we talk to our children all the time why wouldn't our heavenly Father talk to His children?" God does want to talk to us, and He will if we will open our spiritual ears and have faith.

6. "working of miracles" is working more than one miracle and thus adequately covers the plural in the Greek. We realize that although the presence of holy spirit gives each Christian the spiritual power to do healings and miracles, not everyone is called to walk in that kind of ministry. There is a difference between inherent spiritual ability and how that ability will actually be evidenced in the life of an individual Christian. Nevertheless, we assert that many more Christians would be doing healings and miracles if they knew they had the ability and were confident to act on the spiritual power they have.

7. The Greek word translated "discerning" is plural. Nevertheless, we used "discerning" because it has the overtones of plurality. If a person is "discerning," it is because he has exhibited discernment in a multitude of situations.

8. The word "spirits" in the phrase "discerning of spirits" does not refer to "attitudes." Although that is one of the meanings of pneuma, it is not the meaning in this context. There are many very gifted people that are very sensitive and can "read" people and situations very well, but many of them are unsaved. That discernment is a natural ability, just as is native intelligence and other natural abilities.

1st Corinthians 12:7-11- **NIV**
Now to each one the manifestation of the Spirit is given for the common good. 8 To one there is given through the Spirit the message of wisdom, to another the message of knowledge by means of the same Spirit, 9 to another faith by the same Spirit, to another gifts of healing by that one Spirit, 10 to another miraculous powers, to another prophecy, to another distinguishing between spirits, to another speaking in different kinds of tongues, and to still another the interpretation of tongues. 11 All these are the work of one and the same Spirit, and he gives them to each one, just as he determines.

CHAPTER 8

REVELATION GIFTS

These are Gifts that Give a Believer Power to Supernaturally "Know".

These gifts are used by God to REVEAL something through us to others.

1. Wisdom

2. A Word of Knowledge

3. Discerning of Spirits

I'm going to call these "manifestation gifts" because they are supernatural in nature.

The Holy Spirit was present during Jesus' life on earth.

The Holy Spirit was present during each stage of Christ's life. When the angel appeared to Mary, the mother of Jesus, he declared: "The Holy Spirit will come upon you, and the power of the Most High will overshadow you. Therefore, the holy one to be born will be called the Son of God" (Luke 1:35 **NIV**). For unto us a child is born, unto us a son is given, and the government shall be upon his shoulder: and his name shall be called Wonderful, Counsellor, The mighty God, The everlasting Father, The Prince of Peace. (Isaiah 9:6 -**NIV**)

"The Spirit of the Lord is upon me, because he has anointed me to proclaim good news to the poor. He has sent me to proclaim liberty to the captives and recovering of sight to the blind", to set at liberty those who are oppressed, to proclaim the year of the Lord's favour … but he said to them, "I must preach the good news of the kingdom of God to the other towns as well; for I was sent for this purpose." Luke 4:18-19) (Isaiah 61:1-20: **NIV**.

"Jesus said to them, "If God were your Father, you would love me, for I came from God and I am here. I came not of my own accord, but he sent me."

John 8:42: **NIV**

Without a life full of the Holy Spirit, it is impossible to build the body of Christ."

A gospel with no emphasis on the Holy Spirit is flat. In certain moments, when there was a special manifestation of God, the New Testament emphatically states that the partakers were filled with the Holy Spirit. This was the experience of many: John the Baptist was full of the Spirit in his mother's womb (Luke 1:15 **NIV**); Elizabeth, when Mary greeted her (Luke 1:41); and Zechariah, father of John the Baptist, when he prophesied (Luke 1:67). Jesus, filled with the Holy Spirit, was led by the same Spirit into the desert (Luke 4:1). The disciples were filled with the Spirit in the upper room, and Peter, filled with the Holy Spirit, stood up to preach on the day of Pentecost (Acts 2:14). The young Stephen, full of the Spirit, saw the glory of God when he was stoned (Acts 7:55-56 **NIV**); and Paul, inspired by the Spirit, rebuked a sorcerer (Acts 13:9-11). There is no doubt that in the church a life filled with the Holy Spirit should be the norm. The filling of the Holy Spirit was even a requirement for serving in the church. Without a life full of the Holy Spirit, it is impossible to build the body of Christ, and we end up limiting God's work in our lives.

But you will receive power when the Holy Spirit has come on you, and you will be my witnesses in Jerusalem, in all Judea and Samaria, and to the end of the earth'" (Acts 1:7-8 **NIV**).

For over three years, these men had been witnesses of the continual manifestation of God's power through Jesus, and now the doors were being opened for them to access this power that they had so admired.

The disciples also desired the fruit of the Holy Spirit, but for that, it was necessary for them to relate to Him as a person. Before seeing the divine manifestation, the believer will learn to love, serve, adore, and respect the Spirit, wait in Him and form a relationship with Him

The power of the Holy Spirit changes lives.

Acts clearly states how to recognise someone that is full of the Spirit: "Jesus said in Acts 1 v 8 **NIV** 'You will be My witnesses" Love is a distinguishing mark of the disciples, while being a witness distinguishes those who are full of the Spirit. It does not matter how many spiritual experiences one may have, whoever does not testify of Christ does not show evidence of being filled by the Spirit.

If we analyse what Paul says in Galatians 3:2-**NIV**- "I only want to learn this from you: Did you receive the Spirit by the works of the law or by believing what you heard?" we realise that this is a rhetorical question; no one receives the Holy Spirit based on what they do. We experience salvation freely; there is no reason to relate to God differently in our experience with the Holy Spirit. It is also a grace based experience. In the same way that we receive Christ without doubting whether He will enter our lives or not, we should receive the Holy Spirit by faith and believe that He will respond to our requests without delay.

CHAPTER 9

OUR HEAVENLY FATHER GIVES US THE HOLY SPIRIT

Jesus skilfully expresses the essence of this experience: "If you then, who are evil, know how to give good gifts to your children, how much more will the heavenly Father give the Holy Spirit to those who ask him?" (Luke 11:13- **NIV**).

4.   Praying in the Spirit, according to Rom. 8:26-28, **NIV**- brings a good answer to every prayer.

Secondly, the manifestation of the Spirit in our lives is …

B. The way we worship "in the Spirit."

1.   True worship is when we worship the Lord by the Spirit's prompting John 4:23-24- **NIV**.

2.   The manifestation of the Spirit is the physical demonstration unique to each one us whereby the Holy Spirit helps us to glorify Christ in our worship. John 16:14, "Howbeit when he, the Spirit of truth, is come … He shall glorify me: for he shall receive of mine and shall shew it unto you.

3.   When Pentecostal people completely yield to the Spirit during a worship service, powerful things take place.

4. The manifestation of the Spirit is the way the Holy Spirit displays, and we express God's Power in us. What do you do when you are wholly deluged in the power of God? David danced, the lame man leaped, John fell as dead, etc.

In contrary:

Ephesians 4:30 says; "And do not grieve the Holy Spirit of God, by whom you were sealed for the day of redemption." In this case the word grieve is used as a verb, meaning: "to cause to feel grief or sorrow." In other words, the Scripture is exhorting me not to cause the Holy Spirit to feel grief or sorrow as a result of my choices. I grieve the Holy Spirit by not allowing myself to be led by Him but choosing my own way instead. I grieve the Holy Spirit by not obeying Him.

When I realize that I cannot live a life of overcoming sin without the help of the Holy Spirit, it becomes very important to me how I respond to the Holy Spirit when He speaks to me. First of all, I have to listen to His voice!

What does the Holy Spirit do for us?

We live in a fast-paced society, and most of us live a fast-paced lifestyle, with fast travel, fast communication, fast access to a wealth of information, etc. If in the middle of this I do not consciously "set my mind on the things of the Spirit," I will not be able to hear His 'still small voice' in my heart of hearts. When I do not listen to Him, I end up grieving the Holy Spirit, because He has so much to tell me that will bring me joy and happiness and lead me to a life of freedom from sin and self.

Grieving the Holy Spirit by disobedience

Jesus called the Holy Spirit "The Helper," and also said: "When He, the Spirit of truth is come, He will guide you into all truth." John 16:13 **NIV**. All Christians are called to follow in the footsteps of Jesus, He who did not sin. I need to be led step by step because I cannot find the way by myself.

The Spirit will never force me He wants to lead me into a life of victory, the happiest and most fulfilling life a person can ever live. The Holy Spirit will always lead me on a path of humility because He knows that is the only access road to an overcoming life. I grieve the Holy Spirit by not allowing myself to be led but choosing my own way instead.

God gives His Holy Spirit to those who obey Him. The Bible makes it clear that the Holy Spirit and the flesh

Sin is anything that goes against God's will and His laws. To commit sin is to transgress or disobey these laws. The lust to sin dwells in human nature. In other words, it is contaminated and motivated by the sinful …

our human nature are in total opposition to each other. So I cannot live according to my natural inclinations and at the same time obey the Spirit. That is why we read in Ephesians 4:30-31 **NIV**- says, "Do not grieve the Holy Spirit of God … let all bitterness, wrath, anger, loud quarrelling, and evil speaking be put away from you with all malice." I grieve the Holy Spirit by not obeying Him.

I BELIEVE WE HAVE GRIEVED THE HOLY SPIRIT.

The bible says 'do not grieve the Holy Spirit of God',--WE NEED TO REPENT- WE HAVE GRIEVED THE HOLY SPIRIT ... WE NEED TO PLEAD THE BLOOD -OF JESUS UPON OUR LIVES AS WELL AS PLEADING THE MERCY OF GOD- LETS SPEAK MERCY UPON OURSELVES, OUR FAMILY - IN JESUS NAME.

The Bible teaches that we should not grieve the Holy Spirit of God, by whom you were sealed for the day of redemption." In this case the word grieve is used as a verb, meaning: "to cause to feel grief or sorrow." In other words, the Scripture is exhorting me not to cause the Holy Spirit to feel grief or sorrow as a result of my choices. I grieve the Holy Spirit by not allowing myself to be led by Him but choosing my own way instead. I grieve the Holy Spirit by not obeying Him.

Philippians 3:8-21 (**NIV**)
8 What is more, I consider everything a loss because of the surpassing worth of knowing Christ Jesus my Lord, for whose sake I have lost all things. I consider them garbage, that I may gain Christ, 9 and be found in him, not having a righteousness of my own that comes from the law, but that which is through faith in Christ the righteousness that comes from God on the basis of faith. 10 I want to know Christ yes, to know the power of his resurrection and participation in his sufferings, becoming like him in his death, 11 and so, somehow, attaining to the resurrection from the dead.

12 Not that I have already obtained all this, or have already arrived at my goal, but I press on to take hold of that for which Christ Jesus took hold of me. 13 Brothers and sisters, I do not consider myself yet to have taken hold of it. But one thing I do: Forgetting what is behind and straining toward what is ahead, 14 I press on toward the goal to win the prize for which God has called me heavenward in Christ Jesus.

When I realize that I cannot live a life of overcoming sin without the help of the Holy Spirit, it becomes very important to me how I respond to the Holy Spirit when He speaks to me. First of all, I have to listen to His voice!

The root cause of all our spiritual problems lies in our not knowing God as a Loving Father and a Sovereign God. One truth that has revolutionised my Christian life is the glorious revelation that Jesus gave us that the Father loves us just as He loved Him. Jesus prayed to the Father, in John 17: verse 23 **NIV**- I, in them and you in me so that they may be brought to complete unity. Then the world will know that you sent me and have loved them even as you have loved me. Jesus prayed here that the world around us might know this truth. But it has to grip our hearts first, before the world can realise it.

Our world is truly seeing some of the most troubled times of any generation I believe it's because we have grieved the Holy Spirit?

1. Today (in 2019) - UK IS FACING A BREXIT VOTE WHICH IS CRITICAL- Brexit is-

Causing disruption in Parliament – trying to cause trouble and disruption rather that joining forces to get the best deal possible before October 31 October 2018 with regards to Brexit.

2. LGBT school lessons have caused protests to spread nationwide

Mainly Muslim families have been protesting outside Anderton Park Primary School in Birmingham after pupils were given books featuring transgender children and gay families.

(WHERE ARE CHRISTIANS? WHY ARE THEY NOT STANDING UP TO DEFEND OUR CHILDREN)?

In Birmingham (UK), a Protest leader said:

"All we are concerned about; is we are having our children come home with material that contradicts our moral values."

Another Protester said: "It's not about gay lesbian rights and equality. This is purely about proselytising a homosexual way of life to children."

When asked if he believed children could be "recruited to be gay", another protester said: "You can condition them to accept this as being a normal way of life and it makes the children more promiscuous as they grow older."

He added: "Whether they become gay or not, they can still enter into gay relationships.

"They want to convert 'you', they want to convert 'your' morality and that's just wrong."

3.   Let's look at the statistics of Abortions;

In 2017, approximately 206,880 abortions took place in Great Britain = 1 abortion every 2 and half minutes for the entire year 2017.

Be filled with the Spirit (Holy Spirit)! And avoid sin.

Ephesians 5:17-18 Therefore do not be foolish but understand what the Lord's will is 'do not get drunk on wine, which leads to debauchery. Instead, be filled with the Spirit',

4.   Drugs- and -violence (knives and guns) - sending our children to Prisons …

There have been more than 50 murders in different cities in UK, so far this year - and one of the UK, MP says the drugs trade is driving a rise in violence.

"We are the drugs market of Europe," the UK, MP told BBC Radio 4's programme this week. This figure comes from the National Crime Agency, which says that drug trafficking to the UK costs an estimated £10.7 billion per year.

This actually refers to the cost to the public purse of illegal drug use - in treating people in the NHS, the costs to the courts of dealing with offences, thefts by drug users and so on - rather than the worth of the market.

The Home Office has estimated the illegal drugs market to be worth £5.3bn.

5. Suicidal cases-

One UK Student Dies by Suicide Every Four Days – and the Majority are Male. Why? The suicide epidemic at Bristol in the academic year 2017/18 - which claimed six lives - is thought to be the highest number of students killing themselves in one year at a British university.

Many students took their own lives before one girl (*not real names*) Cathy, and Ben were found five days after they died.

Cathy's parents Tilly and Molly - who are suing the university - have made a BBC One documentary, dying for a Degree, as they search for answers over why so many students are dying. But Cathy's mum revealed at her daughter's inquest earlier this month that by the end of her first year she was already struggling.

Although she was "bright" and had never "failed academically" in her life, there were other students performing better, and she was "disappointed" with her 60 per cent mark for that year.

After a summer spent with new boyfriend Ben, who attended University of Gloucestershire, she moved into a Bristol flat with two course mates. Peter and John

Tilly and Molly now believe Cathy (*not real names*), who previously suffered from acute social anxiety, began to experience a decline in her mental health at the end 2017, causing her grades to suffer.

Staff at the School of Physics became aware that she was skipping her one-to-one interviews and would suffer from panic attacks and become unable to speak and have to leave the room.

"She knew she had bad marks, she knew she might fail the module and she knew she might well be kicked off the course," explains her father in the documentary. Ten weeks before her death, Cathy (*not real name*) tried to seek help by sending an email in the early hours to student administration manager Alex (*not his real name*).

She wrote: "I wanted to tell you that the last few days have been really hard. I've been having suicidal thoughts and to a certain degree have attempted it.

"I want help to go to the student health clinic or wherever you think I should go to help me through this and I would like somebody to go with me as I will find it very hard to talk to people about these issues."

Later that day, a friend took her to the university GP who recorded she had made a suicide attempt of "definite intent" and was "in a state of acute distress" and "at high risk of ending her life given her presentation". On the day she died Cathy- (*not real name*) who had social anxiety - was due to give a presentation in front of 43 fellow students and two staff[2]

6. Fornication is a serious sin that can exclude us from heaven

In today's post (2019). I will focus on the sin of fornication and present the clear biblical teaching against it. Sadly, many Churches preach very little or let's say 'nothing' is heard from the pulpit or in the classroom about this issue of fornication. The hope in this post today is to present a resounding, biblical trumpet call to purity that leaves no doubt as to the sinfulness of sex before marriage. Scripture is clear: fornicators will not inherit the Kingdom of God. That is to say, fornication is a mortal sin and those who do not repent of it will go to Hell.

7. There has been riots in HONGKONG FOR WEEKS NOW- MID 2019.

8. THE ASIAN WORLD AND MOST WORLDS HAVE RELIGIOUS CRISIS AND POLITICAL CRISIS.

IS THERE NO MORE MERCY LEFT FOR US. WE NEED TO SING SONGS OF VICTORY NOT ONLY FOR TROUBLED NATIONS:

9. The political conflicts, strange weather patterns, economic turmoil in every part of the world. There has never been a time when covenant understanding was vital to God 's children than now .

10. Rejection, bitterness and betrayal:

---

[2] https://www.thesun.co.uk/news/9168417/parents-bristol-student-killed-university-suicide-epidemic/

2 Timothy 4 v 10 **NIV**- for Demas, because he loved this world, has deserted me and has gone to Thessalonica Crescens has gone to Galatia, and Titus to Dalmatia. Having loved this present world,

not the sins and corruptions of the world, the lust of the flesh, the lust of the eyes, and the pride of life; such a love is inconsistent with the love of the Father and the grace of God; nor an immoderate love of worldly substance, or of money, which is the root of all evil; but a love of life, or of a longer life in this present world; he was desirous of living longer in this world, and chose not to hazard his life by staying with the apostle, a prisoner at Rome; and therefore left him, and provided for his own safety and security: and is departed unto Thessalonica: which perhaps was his native country; and however he was at a sufficient distance from Rome, where he might judge himself safe; and if he was a worldly and earthly minded man, this was a fit place for him, being a place of trade and business: and this doubtless gave rise to a tradition, that he afterwards became a priest of the idol gods among the Thessalonians

The saints need to know that we are not alone in all this, that our God is bigger than what faces us. That in spite of our frailties and short comings, His compassion fails not. That in wrath our father remembers mercies. That those who are for us are more than those who are against us.

11. America is in trouble. From sea to shining sea we are witnessing the devolution of a nation. The United States is quickly becoming the divided states. Disunity and conflict abound. Family breakdown, the immigration crisis, the threat of terrorism, an abiding racial divide and political dysfunction all point to a deeper problem.

Regardless of which side of the political aisle you sit on, it is clear: Things are unravelling at warp speed. Like never before, we must pray for our nation and her leaders.

The future of our culture is in the hands of Christians because the cause of our cultural demise is innately spiritual. And if a problem is spiritual, its cure must be spiritual as well. If we Christians are going to help turn our nation to God, we must fall on our knees and our faces before God and pray. We must not only talk about prayer but pray. Not only agree on the importance of prayer but pray. Not only preach on the power of prayer, but pray. As One Preacher once said, "To get our nation on its feet, we must get on our knees."

Second Chronicles 7:14 contains an awesome promise: "If My people who are called by My name will humble themselves, and pray and seek My face, and turn from their wicked ways, then I will hear from heaven, and will forgive their sin and heal their land." In this hallmark passage, God calls a nation to pray.

Prayer is an earthly request for heavenly intervention. It is the tool and strategy we have been given in order to pull something down out of the invisible and into the visible. Prayer enacts God's hand in history like nothing else because prayer is relational communication with God.

But we can't enjoy this kind of divine intervention of healing in our land with just a little prayer tossed toward Heaven occasionally. The kind of prayer that will reclaim lives, families and a nation for God must take high priority in our schedules. In fact, if you look back at Nehemiah 1:4, you see that Nehemiah prayed and fasted for days when he heard about the conditions in Jerusalem.

In the face of his nation's ongoing cultural demise, Nehemiah didn't sit down and write out a "Great Society" program for Jerusalem. He didn't propose a Jerusalem "New Deal." He fasted and prayed and sought God. As he did so, God revealed His strategy and reversed years of deterioration in just 52 days. This is because prayer saves time.

We know that God moved in response to Nehemiah's prayer, allowing him to use his position of influence with the king to get Artaxerxes to support the rebuilding of Jerusalem. But Nehemiah didn't start with his position. He started with prayer providing the link between God, Nehemiah's problem and his position.

If you see something in our nation or political leaders that is broken, is prayer the first thing you do, or the last thing you do? If it's the last thing you do, more than likely you will have wasted your time on other things. If prayer comes last, then so will the solution to the problem.

God does not like being last.

If we are going to turn our communities and nation around, congregations are going to have to join in a unified, national solemn assembly (Joel 1:14) to repent and to throw themselves before the face of Almighty God.

We could save a lot of time and worry if we spent time praying first. In Nehemiah's case, the crumbled walls of Jerusalem were a pressing problem, something that cried out for immediate and decisive action.

But Nehemiah fasted and prayed first. So my question to you is, "What wall is crumbling?" The answer: America. The spiritual foundations of this nation are crumbling fast; our beloved nation is imploding. But political action won't stop the erosion. More money and finger pointing and judgment won't stop it. Instead, political leaders need our fasting and our prayers.

In Isaiah 58, the prophet gives us the benefits of fasting God's way. As you read it, notice the conditional statements in it the "if/then" logic that clearly lays out for us what we are to do "if" we want to experience the "then." When we fast with intentional love:

"Then your light will break out like the dawn, and your recovery will speedily spring forth; and your righteousness will go before you; The glory of the Lord will be your rear guard. Then you will call, and the Lord will answer; You will cry, and He will say, 'Here I am.' If you remove the yoke from your midst, the pointing of the finger and speaking wickedness, and if you give yourself to the hungry and satisfy the desire of the afflicted, then your light will rise in darkness and your gloom will become like midday. And the Lord will continually guide you and satisfy your desire in scorched places and give strength to your bones; and you will be like a watered garden, and like a spring of water whose waters do not fail. Those from among you will rebuild the ancient ruins; You will raise up the age-old foundations; and you will be called the repairer of the breach, the restorer of the streets in which to dwell" (Isaiah 58:8-12, NASB).

Do we want the light of the Body of Christ to break out like the dawn across our nation? Do we want our country to experience a speedy recovery from what ails it? Do we want the Lord to answer us when we call on Him on behalf of our communities? Do we want God's guidance?

If the answer is "Yes," then we have to do the "if" that comes before the "then." It's dependent on that. Because the praying and fasting that will get God's attention is one that involves loving others in both word and action. It means winning people to Jesus Christ with compassion and kindness.

God's fast isn't merely skipping a meal or saying a prayer although those things are crucial. To impact our country for good and turn our nation to God, we His people must fast and pray with His heart. For only when we have His heart will we invoke His hand. And we must do this together.

Think of the impact we could have as the Body of Christ if we would seek God's face in prayer and fasting on behalf of our nation and political leaders in a unified way. Biblical unity is oneness of purpose. It is not uniformity. Unity means moving together toward the same goal.

The clearest antithesis of this, frustrates on how churches would come together for the sake of evangelism, but then go back to their own disconnected corners after the event has ended.

As a result, their collective impact was truncated. Unfortunately, we've allowed the separations in politics, power, culture and preferences to create a separation among churches as well. Because of that, we are making little visible difference in our nation.

There are more churches and non-profit parachurch organisations in our country than ever before. What if we joined together, on our knees, toward a shared purpose or vision to make a collective spiritual impact on our nation's problems?

It is time, now, to set our personal agendas, brands and voices aside and join our hearts and hands in a national solemn assembly to seek God's heart and His hand on behalf of our land.

As Christians, we must ask: Are we going to sit by and watch our culture fall apart and our families disintegrate? Or are we going to do something to help turn America to God?

We are inviting you to not just sing, but songs of victory as we wail. WE SING AND WAIL TODAY NOT ONLY FOR ONE NATION,TODAY.

HOW WOULD JESUS BE PRAYING AND INTERCEDING IF HE WAS IN YOUR CITY BASED ON ALL THE INTERNATIONAL TURMOIL'S.

WE ARE GOD'S PRIESTS AND KINGS. WE ARE CALLED TO MAKE A DIFFERENCE ON OUR KNEES WHEREVER WE ARE. (LETS GET ON OUR KNEES AND ASK THE HOLY SPIRIT FOY HELP.!

CHAPTER 11

DARE TO BELIEVE THAT GOD LOVES YOU JUST AS HE LOVES JESUS

All Christians believe theoretically in a loving Father in heaven. But the fact that they are often worried and anxious and so full of insecurity and fear, proves that they don't believe it deep down in their hearts. There are fewer still who would dare to believe that God loves them AS MUCH AS HE LOVES JESUS! None of us could dare to believe such a truth if Jesus had not plainly told us that it was so. Once your eyes are opened to this glorious truth, it will change your whole outlook on life.

All murmuring and depression and gloom will vanish from your life altogether. I know this can happen, for it happened in my life. This is now the unshakable foundation of my life: GOD LOVES ME JUST AS HE LOVES JESUS. It's not because you don't fast and pray sufficiently that you are not entering the victorious life. Victory comes, not through self-effort but through faith. "Faith in what?", you may ask. Faith in God's perfect love for you. Many believers live under the condemnation of Satan who keeps telling them, "You are not fasting enough. You are not praying enough. You are not witnessing enough. You are not studying the Bible enough", etc., etc., They are constantly being whipped up by such thoughts into an endless round of activity and into a multitude of dead works. Do you realise that all your self- discipline, fasting, praying, tithing and witnessing are dead works, if they do not originate in love for God? And they cannot originate in love unless you are secure in God's love first. Paul's prayer for the Christians at Ephesus was that they might be rooted and grounded in the love of God. (Ephesians 3:16,17 **NIV**).

The world is full of people who are looking for someone to love them. Many Christians go from church to church, wanting to be loved. Some seek for love in friendships and some in marriage. But all this search can end in disappointment. Like orphans, the children of Adam are insecure and as a result are again and again overcome by bouts of self-pity. The sad thing is that even after conversion, many still remain insecure, when there is no need for them to be so. What is the answer of the gospel to this problem? The answer is to find our security in the love of God. Jesus repeatedly told His disciples that the hairs on their head were all numbered and that a God Who fed the millions of birds and clothed the millions of flowers would certainly take care of them. A greater argument than all of that, is: "He who did not spare His own Son but gave Him up freely for us, how shall He not with Him also freely give us ALL THINGS " (Rom. 8:32). As God cared for Jesus, He will care for you too.

One reason why God allows us at times to be disappointed with our fellow human beings is so that we might learn to stop leaning on man. He desires to free us from such idolatry (for it is a form of idolatry to depend on man), so that we might learn to lean wholly upon Him alone. And so, when God orders your circumstances in such a way that you are disappointed on every side, that shouldn't discourage you. It is just God weaning you away from the arm of flesh so that you might learn to live by faith in Him. Learn to find your security in the fact that God loves you as He loved Jesus. All competition and jealousy among Christians rises out of this same insecurity. A man who is secure in the love of God and who believes that God made no mistake in making him the way He made him, and in giving him the gifts and talents He gave him, can never possibly be jealous of another or compete with another. All problems of relationships among believers are also basically due to this same insecurity. Just think how many of your problems will be solved when your eyes are opened to this one truth - that God loves you exactly as He loves Jesus.

CHAPTER 12

ALL BELIEVERS OUGHT TO PRAY FOR SINNERS TO REPENT

1 John 5:20 … 19 We know that we are of God, and that the whole world is under the power of the evil one. 20 And we know that the Son of God has come and has given us understanding, so that we may know Him who is true; and we are in Him who is true in His Son Jesus Christ. He is the TRUE God and eternal life.

ONE DAY WE CALLED A GROUP OF WOMEN TO PRAY FOR CHILDREN WHO WERE TRAPPED IN A CAVE IN THAILAND AND BELIEVED GOD. WE SAW GOD MOVE NATIONS TO RESCUE THE CHILDREN.

GOD HEARS US WHEN WE PRAY. WHEREVER WE ARE. GOD HONOURS PRAYING SAINTS AS THEY PRAY. WE HAVE THE MANDATE AND WE WILL JUST RAISE A VOICE OF WORSHIP TO OUR GOD -OUR FATHER

Fornication is a Serious Sin that Can Exclude Us From Heaven

In today's post (2019) I will focus on the sin of fornication and present the clear biblical teaching against it. Sadly, many Catholics report that little to nothing is heard from the pulpit or in the classroom about this issue. The hope in this post today is to present a resounding, biblical trumpet call to purity that leaves no doubt as to the sinfulness of sex before marriage. Scripture is clear: fornicators will not inherit the Kingdom of God. That is to say, fornication is a mortal sin and those who do not repent of it, will go to Hell.

Isaiah 66:6-9 KJV

A voice of noise from the city, a voice from the temple, a voice of the Lord that rendered recompense to his enemies. 7 Before she travailed, she brought forth; before her pain came, she was delivered of a man child. 8 Who hath heard such a thing? who hath seen such things? Shall the earth be made to bring forth in one day? or shall a nation be born at once? for as soon as Zion travailed, she brought forth her children. 9 Shall I bring to the birth, and not cause to bring forth? saith the Lord: shall I cause to bring forth and shut the womb? saith thy God.

Isaiah 49:22-26 KJV

Thus, saith the Lord God, Behold, I will lift up mine hand to the Gentiles, and set up my standard to the people: and they shall bring thy sons in their arms, and thy daughters shall be carried upon their shoulders. 23 And kings shall be thy nursing fathers, and their queens thy nursing mothers: they shall bow down to thee with their face toward the earth, and lick up the dust of thy feet; and thou shalt know that I am the Lord : for they shall not be ashamed that wait for me.

24 Shall the prey be taken from the mighty, or the lawful captive delivered? 25 But thus saith the Lord, Even the captives of the mighty shall be taken away, and the prey of the terrible shall be delivered: for I will contend with him that contended with thee, and I will save thy children.

26 And I will feed them that oppress thee with their own flesh; and they shall be drunken with their own blood, as with sweet wine: and all flesh shall know that I the Lord am thy Saviour and thy Redeemer, the mighty One of Jacob.

CHAPTER 13

OVERCOME SIN BY THE HOLY SPIRIT

The good news is that the Holy Spirit is also the One who gives me power to obey and power to overcome all these tendencies in my nature! When God sees my sincere desire to obey Him, He will send His Holy Spirit to help me do just that. Jesus told His disciples that they would receive power when the Holy Spirit came upon them. Just like a thirsty person in the desert drinks deeply from a spring of fresh water, I must drink deeply of God's Holy Spirit be filled with His Spirit if I want to live an abundant Christian life.

God's Spirit is in His Word. When I drink deeply of this fountain and of the spirit of faith that is in the Word, I will have power in temptation to overcome sin and do God's will instead of my own. I grieve the Holy Spirit by wandering around in the desert of my own thoughts and ways, too busy or too lazy to drink from the fountain of faith and power that is in God's Word.

But grieving the Holy Spirit is totally unnecessary! He knows that we are weak, and that we don't even know what to pray for in the right way, but He is there to help us in our need, and to pray for us so that we can find God's will and do it. (Romans 8:26-27 NIV) Then we will truly experience the comfort of the Holy Spirit as well as His power.

1. Pentecost reveals the work of a triune God in our salvation.

Pentecost is the day when God clearly demonstrates that salvation and redemption are the work of the triune God. The Father is the source, the initiator, and the final goal of all the redemptive acts of God. The Son is the embodiment of the mission of God. The work of salvation is accomplished through His birth, life, death, resurrection, and ascension. The Holy Spirit is the empowering presence of God who makes us holy.

2. Through the events on Pentecost, the Holy Spirit now dwells among us.

The Holy Spirit is God Himself acting in this world and in our lives. He draws us by His grace to the Father. He intercedes with us and within us, helping us to pray. The Holy Spirit teaches and admonishes us when we read Scripture. He gives us the gift of discernment so that we might have the mind of Christ and think about things in ways that are informed by godly wisdom. He applies and nurtures the fruit of the Spirit in our lives (love, joy, peace, patience, goodness, kindness, gentleness, faithfulness, and self-control). The Holy Spirit assures us of our forgiveness and our adoption as the children of God. In short, the Holy Spirit mediates the presence of God in our lives and in the church.

3. The Holy Spirit empowers the church for effective service, witness, and global mission.

Jesus promised that the Holy Spirit would empower us to be His witnesses to the ends of the earth (Acts 1:8). It is the Holy Spirit who enables the church to serve sacrificially and to be an effective witness unto Christ and the gospel. Holiness, as we shall see, is not just about making us personally righteous, but it is about extending God's glory and righteousness to all peoples of the world! There are thousands of people groups who still have not received the good news about Jesus Christ. It is the Holy Spirit who makes sure that the gospel is proclaimed to the ends of the earth through the empowered witness of the church.

4. The Holy Spirit reveals the signs and wonders of God's in-breaking kingdom.

Fourth, the Holy Spirit is the One who continues to manifest redemptive signs of God's kingdom breaking into the world. The good news of God's powerful work in this world did not stop at the cross and resurrection of Jesus Christ. It is too small to think that we are called to simply proclaim something that happened in history thousands of years ago. While the cross and resurrection form the central proclamation of the church, we also acknowledge that the good news of God's reign continues to unfold. All the future realities of heaven (healing, forgiveness, reconciliation, deliverance from evil, and so forth) are breaking into the world now through the presence of the Holy Spirit. Men and women are healed by the power of the Holy Spirit. They experience forgiveness and reconciliation with one another. The poor and downcast receive hope. The Holy Spirit applies all the future realities of the New Creation to the present. This process will not be fully complete until Jesus returns, but if we look around, we can see that God is still at work by His Spirit, reconciling the world to Himself.

5. The Holy Spirit makes us holy.

Fifth, the Holy Spirit is the One who makes us holy. The presence of the Holy Spirit, God's empowering presence in us, leads to transformational holiness in our lives, in society, and in the world. As God's empowering presence, the Holy Spirit embodies the New Creation, including purity of holiness. This should really begin to expand our understanding of the full dimensions of holiness in our lives. In chapter 4, we saw that holiness is the sign and seal of God's presence in the world. This means that we must expand our ideas regarding what it means for God's holiness to be reintroduced into the world.

We mostly think of it in terms of personal holiness. We understand God's presence as eradicating sin in our lives. This is an important aspect of holiness. However, God's presence also challenges and transforms the society we live in. In other words, social holiness is also crucial to a proper understanding of biblical holiness. God's transformative work infuses not only our individual lives, but also the whole structure of culture and society. Moreover, holiness is not only personal and social; it is also missional. This means that holiness is not just about our being transformed, or even our culture reflecting certain things, but it causes us to think missionally about the world and how we can mirror God's actions in the world.

Colossians 1:17-18 (**NIV**)
17 He is before all things, and in him all things hold together. 18 And he is the head of the body, the church; he is the beginning and the firstborn from among the dead, so that in everything he might have the supremacy.

We pray for revelation to understand how much God loves us He has given us Life, The Holy Spirit and spiritual gifts.

CHAPTER 14

LET YOUR LIVING WATER FLOW

Song lyrics … …

Let your living water flow over my soul

Let your holy spirit come and take control

Of every situation that has troubled my mind

All my cares and burdens unto you I roll

Jesus, Jesus, Jesus

Sing to the Father

Father, Father, Father

Spirit, Spirit, Spirit

CHAPTER 15

JESUS WAS LED AROUND BY THE SPIRIT

Luke 4:1- **NIV**) Jesus, full of the Holy Spirit, returned from the Jordan and was led around by the Spirit in the wilderness

(Mark 5:30- **NIV**) And Jesus immediately knowing in himself that virtue (power) had gone out of him, turned him about in the press, and said, who touched my clothes? Doesn't being "full of the Spirit" or having "virtue (power) gone OUT of Him" sound like the Spirit was in Him?

Even if one says "no," we can see clearly over and over that Jesus did depend on the "power" of the Holy Spirit.

(Acts 10:38) (**NASB**) You know of Jesus of Nazareth, how God anointed Him with the Holy Spirit and with power, and how He went about doing good and healing all who were oppressed by the devil, for God was with Him.

(Lk 4:14- **NIV**) And Jesus returned in the power of the Spirit into Galilee: and there went out a fame of him through all the region round about.

(Lk 5:17- **NIV**) And it came to pass on a certain day, as he was teaching, that there were Pharisees and doctors of the law sitting by, which were come out of every town of Galilee, and Judaea, and Jerusalem: and the power of the Lord was present to heal them.

(Matthew 12:28 **NIV**) But if I cast out devils by the Spirit of God, then the kingdom of God is come unto you.

While Jesus was on Earth, He was fully God AND fully man. However, He voluntarily "veiled" some of His divine attributes (Philippians 2:5-8) (2 Corinthians 8:9) (John 17:4-5). This being the case, it makes perfect sense that He would have depended on the power of the Holy Spirit throughout His ministry on Earth, just as is indicated above. We are told in (Luke 1:15) that John the Baptist was "filled with the Holy Spirit while yet in his mother's womb." If he was filled, isn't it reasonable to believe that Jesus was filled as well during His whole life (some believe it wasn't until His baptism)?

So, yes, I do believe the Holy Spirit lived in Jesus, and I also believe that He depended on the power of the Holy Spirit throughout His life, just Christians are to do today. However, (John 3:34) seems to indicate He had a greater measure of the Holy Spirit than we will ever have.

Holy Spirit
The Holy Spirit has always been present with us since the universe was created (Genesis 1:2). He was present during the time of King David and when Jesus was here.

… when He comes, (The Holy Spirit) will convict the world concerning sin, and righteousness, and judgment; concerning sin, because they do not believe in Me; and concerning righteousness, because I go to the Father, and you no longer behold Me; and concerning judgment, because the ruler of this world has been judged. (**NASB**) John 16:8-11

And they were all filled with the Holy Spirit and began to speak with other tongues, as the Spirit was giving them utterance. (**NASB**) Acts 2:4

So what changed with the Holy Spirit at Pentecost (i.e., at the birth of the Church)?

The Holy Spirit was already with the Apostles, but Jesus said that He would soon come to live inside them (John 14:16-17). Realize, the Holy Spirit in one dimension had always been present with the Apostles on Earth. However, while Jesus was on Earth, He came in a different dimension to be with them for power to do the works of Jesus (Matthew 10:5-8).

Furthermore, on the day of Pentecost, the great mystery is revealed – God has planned to come and "tabernacle" within reborn man! (Colossians 1:27) However, Jesus also said the Holy Spirit would come upon the Apostles at this time, too (Luke 24:49 and Acts 1:8)- (**NIV**)

The Holy Spirit was already with the Apostles, and then at Pentecost, He came within them and upon them. He came within them to cause their spirit that was dead to God to be reborn (Ezekiel 36:26-27). He then took up residence in their spirit to cause their transformation into Christlikeness (1) as they yielded to Him (1 Corinthians 6:19). This is the growing of the fruit of the Spirit in our lives (John 7:37-39. Galatians 5:22,23).

The Holy Spirit then came upon the Apostles to empower them to continue the ministry of Jesus – destroying the works of the devil! (Luke 4:18,19. Acts 1:8)

Does the Holy Spirit always come within (in one dimension) and upon (in a different dimension) a Christian simultaneously today?

Looking at the book of Acts there is a precedence for the Holy Spirit coming within and upon new believers simultaneously at Pentecost (first Jews reborn) (Acts 2:1-4) and at Cornelius' house (first Gentiles or non-Jews reborn) (Acts 10:44-48. Acts 11:15-17). After that, it appears that some received the Holy Spirit within them first but later received the Holy Spirit upon them (Acts 8:12-17. Acts 19:1-6). Therefore, both simultaneously and as separate events are possible today.

Consequently, it is possible to be born again with all of the Holy Spirit living inside you in one dimension yet not have the Holy Spirit in a different dimension upon you. Being born again is our "ticket to heaven," and the Holy Spirit will inculcate Christlikeness in our lives if we yield to His guidance. However, it is having the Holy Spirit upon us that will empower for the most effective ministry.

How do you know if the Holy Spirit is upon you?

This may be the first time you have heard of the Holy Spirit coming upon you similar to those in that heard this for the first time in the book of Acts (Acts 9:17. Acts 8:12-17. Acts 19:1-6).

CHAPTER 16

DO YOU KNOW IF YOU ARE GOING TO HEAVEN WHEN YOU DIE?

How do you know? In the same way, do you know if the Holy Spirit has come upon you? You can know this just as real as you know you are saved. If you are not sure, then accept the Lord Jesus as Saviour (1) (if not already saved) and ask for the Holy Spirit to come upon you.

Remember that you get all of the Holy Spirit in one dimension (1) when you are saved and then grow to voluntarily allow the Holy Spirit to have all of you - which is the journey to transformation into Christlikeness. However, you may still not have the Holy Spirit upon you in this journey to Christlikeness. Again, if you do not know if the Holy Spirit is upon you then ask! (Luke 11:13. Acts 5:32)

Is the promise of the Holy Spirit coming upon the believer for today?

Yes, for all that will answer the Lord's call to repentance! (Acts 2:38,39)

What does the expression "filled with the Holy Spirit" mean? (Luke 4:1. Acts 2:4. Acts 4:8. Acts 4:31. Acts 13:52. Ephesians 5:18)

The expression filled with the Holy Spirit speaks of the Spirit completely influencing the mind and spiritual heart of the believer. The result is that the Holy Spirit leads the Christian's mind and spiritual heart. Realize that the Holy Spirit is not a substance to fill an empty receptacle; He is a Person to lead another person, the believer. He does not fill a Christian's life with Himself like you fill your gas tank with gas nor does He control a person like a robot against their will.

Furthermore, the Holy Spirit does not automatically lead the believer just because He indwells him. The influence that the Holy Spirit exerts over the believer is dependent upon the believer's active and correct adjustment to the Spirit. The Lord Jesus did not save us until we recognized Him as the Saviour.

Why did the Holy Spirit descend from Heaven like a dove to rest on Jesus if He was already here? (John 1:32 **NIV**)

The Holy Spirit is God and is not confined to the narrow concept of time and space that we have in our lives on Earth. He exists in one dimension everywhere in the universe simultaneously (Psalms 139:7,8). However, He came in a different dimension to rest upon Jesus in the form of a Dove (1). The Holy Spirit came upon Jesus to empower Him for ministry (Luke 4:14,17,18,19). Remember, Jesus emptied Himself (1) of self (i.e., His right to all that being God entails) before being born of the Virgin Mary (Philippians 2:6,7). Consequently, the miracles performed by Jesus were done in the power of God the Holy Spirit not in Jesus' power as God (Acts 10:38). Again, Jesus was very God of God when He walked the Earth; however, He had voluntarily "emptied" Himself of the right to use His power as God. He came to earth as "son of man" empowered by the Holy Spirit to destroy the works of the devil (1 John 3:8. Hebrews 2:14).

So, what changed with the Holy Spirit at Pentecost (i.e., at the birth of the Church)?

The Holy Spirit was already with the Apostles, but Jesus said that He would soon come to live inside them (John 14:16-17). Realize, the Holy Spirit in one dimension had always been present with the Apostles on Earth. However, while Jesus was on Earth, He came in a different dimension to be with them for power to do the works of Jesus (Matthew 10:5-8).

Furthermore, on the day of Pentecost, the great mystery is revealed – God has planned to come and "tabernacle" within reborn man! (Colossians 1:27) However, Jesus also said the Holy Spirit would come upon the Apostles at this time, too (Luke 24:49. Acts 1:8)- **NIV**

The Holy Spirit was already with the Apostles, and then at Pentecost, He came within them and upon them. He came within them to cause their spirit that was dead to God to be reborn (Ezekiel 36:26-27). He then took up residence in their spirit to cause their transformation into Christlikeness (1) as they yielded to Him (1 Corinthians 6:19). This is the growing of the fruit of the Spirit in our lives (John 7:37-39. Galatians 5:22,23).

The Holy Spirit then came upon the Apostles to empower them to continue the ministry of Jesus – destroying the works of the devil! (Luke 4:18,19. Acts 1:8)

Does the Holy Spirit always come within (in one dimension) and upon (in a different dimension) a Christian simultaneously today?

Looking at the book of Acts there is a precedence for the Holy Spirit coming within and upon new believers simultaneously at Pentecost (first Jews reborn) (Acts 2:1-4) and at Cornelius' house (first Gentiles or non-Jews reborn) (Acts 10:44-48. Acts 11:15-17). After that, it appears that some received the Holy Spirit within them first but later received the Holy Spirit upon them (Acts 8:12-17. Acts 19:1-6). Therefore, both simultaneously and as separate events are possible today.

Consequently, it is possible to be born again with all of the Holy Spirit living inside you in one dimension yet not have the Holy Spirit in a different dimension upon you. Being born again is our "ticket to heaven, " and the Holy Spirit will inculcate Christlikeness in our lives if we yield to His guidance. However, it is having the Holy Spirit upon us that will empower for the most effective ministry (Acts 1:8).

How do you know if the Holy Spirit is upon you?

This may be the first time you have heard of the Holy Spirit coming upon you similar to those in that heard this for the first time in the book of Acts (Acts 9:17. Acts 8:12-17. Acts 19:1-6).

Do you know if you are going to Heaven if you die? How do you know? In the same way, do you know if the Holy Spirit has come upon you? You can know this just as real as you know you are saved. If you are not sure, then accept the Lord Jesus as Saviour (1) (if not already saved) and ask for the Holy Spirit to come upon you.

Remember that you get all of the Holy Spirit in one dimension (1) when you are saved and then grow to voluntarily allow the Holy Spirit to have all of you - which is the journey to transformation into Christlikeness. However, you may still not have the Holy Spirit upon you in this journey to Christlikeness. Again, if you do not know if the Holy Spirit is upon you then ask for the Holy Spirit to come upon you.

Is the promise of the Holy Spirit coming upon the believer for today?

Yes, for all that will answer the Lord's call to repentance! (Acts 2:38,39)

What does the expression "filled with the Holy Spirit" mean?

The expression 'filled with the Holy Spirit' 'speaks of the Spirit completely influencing the mind and spiritual heart of the believer'. The result is that the Holy Spirit leads the Christian's mind and spiritual heart. Realise that the Holy Spirit is not a substance to fill an empty receptacle; He is a Person to lead another person, the believer. He does not fill a Christian's life with Himself like you fill your gas tank with gas nor does He control a person like a robot against their will.

Furthermore, the Holy Spirit does not automatically lead the believer just because He indwells him. The influence that the Holy Spirit exerts over the believer is dependent upon the believer's active and correct adjustment to the Spirit. The Lord Jesus did not save us until we recognized Him as the Saviour and put our trust in Him for salvation. Likewise, the Holy Spirit does not lead us in the sense of permeating our will, mind, and emotions, until we recognize Him as the One who has been sent by the Father (at Jesus' request - John 15:26) to sanctify our lives, and trust Him to perform His ministry in and through us.

There must be an ever-present conscious dependence upon and definite subjection to the Holy Spirit, a constant yielding to His ministry and lean upon Him for guidance and power if He is to lead the believer in the most efficient manner and with the largest and best results.

Furthermore, this leading will not transpire without sincere desire (Matthew 5:6. Romans 14:17). Again, the Holy Spirit does not control a person but rather develops the self-control of a person such that they can voluntarily choose by an act of their will to follow Him unreservedly (Galatians 5:22, 23) **NIV.** Furthermore, to be constantly under the influence of the Holy Spirit is God's plan for the normal Christian way of life!

CHAPTER 17

WHAT DOES THE TERM "BAPTIZED" WITH THE HOLY SPIRIT MEAN?

To baptize means - to place into. Jesus baptizes - places us into - the Holy Spirit (Matthew 3:11. Mark 1:8. Luke 3:16. John 1:33). The first people to be baptized with the Holy Spirit, by reason of Jesus' request to the Father (John 14:16. John 15:26. Acts 2:33), were the approximately 120 waiting in Jerusalem on the day of Pentecost including Mary Jesus' mother (Acts 1:4. Acts 1:12-15). The Holy Spirit came into the room and filled it with Himself (Acts 2:1,2). Therefore, they were placed into or baptized in the Holy Spirit (Acts 11:16) and the Holy Spirit came within them (1 Corinthians 12:13).

We typically think of baptism as taking a person and lowering them into a container full of water until they are completely immersed. However, the same effect could be had by having a person stand in an empty container and then fill the container with water until they are completely immersed or baptized. The latter better describes what happened on the Day of Pentecost as the Holy Spirit filled the room thus immersing or baptizing everyone present with Himself!

The Holy Spirit baptized or immersed them in Himself causing their dead (to God) spirits to be replaced with a new perfect spirit (1)(Ezekiel 36:26,27. 1 Corinthians 6:11. Hebrews 12:23). This is part of the mystery of the Body of Christ - the Holy Spirit or Spirit of Christ comes inside us to join us all together with Jesus as our Head (Romans 8:9).

Please allow me to go on record here to state that this in no way makes us God. We are the creation and He the triune God is the creator.

That is, the Baptism in the Holy Spirit is when we are born again, placed into the Body of Christ, and the Holy Spirit indwells us (1 Corinthians 12:13. Ephesians 4:4-6. 1 Corinthians 6:19).

Therefore, the following terms can be considered synonymous:

Holy Spirit "within" a person(s)

Holy Spirit "baptizing" a person(s)

What does the term "anointed" with the Holy Spirit mean?

Jesus stated that the "anointing with the Holy Spirit" is synonymous with the "Holy Spirit coming upon" someone (Luke 4:18. Luke 3:21-23). Furthermore, Luke in the book of Acts identifies that this anointing with the Holy Spirit is what gave Jesus the power to do the works of God (Acts 10:38). It was the works of God done by Jesus that was the proof positive that God sent Him (John 5:36).

Jesus states that the Holy Spirit will come upon us to give us the power to continue His works (Acts 1:8). These works are to be one of the proofs to the World that Jesus has sent us (John 14:11,12).

Therefore, the following terms can be considered synonymous:

Holy Spirit "upon" a person(s)

Holy Spirit "anointing" a person(s)

Realize, all that are born again have the anointing within them in the person of the Holy Spirit that dwells in our reborn perfect spirits (1 John 2:20,27. 2 Corinthians 1:21,22). However, not all that are born again have asked God for this anointing to be released to come upon them to give them the power for a much more effective ministry (1). That is, God does not have to send the Holy Spirit down from Heaven when you ask Him for the Holy Spirit to come upon or anoint you for ministry because He already dwells within a believer's reborn spirit! (John 7:37-39)

What about the anointing of the Holy Spirit today?

I believe the Holy Spirit comes upon or anoints people separated by time (i.e … the time from when they were born again, and He came within or rather baptized them in Himself) today more than He does simultaneously. This is likely due to our ignorance of the Holy Spirit's ministry today just like in the later chapters of the book of Acts (Acts 19:1-6). However, be of good cheer – it is never too late! Realize, you will never be as effective in ministry or have the power to lead a holy life without the Holy Spirit both in and upon you (Galatians 5:16).

Steps to having the Holy Spirit come upon you (or receiving the anointing of the Holy Spirit):

I. We must have accepted Jesus as our Lord and Saviour. This should lead to a public confession of our renunciation of sin and our acceptance of Jesus (Acts 2:38,39). To repent is to change your mind. Change your mind from an attitude that rejects Jesus Christ to one that accepts Him as Saviour, Lord, and King. Water immersion is the way public confession was done in the scriptures (Acts 2:38) as is the Biblical command for today (Matthew 28:19).

II. We must completely surrender every area of our lives to God (Acts 5:32). This includes letting go of all sin(s). Ask God to search your spiritual heart for sin (Psalms 139:23,24). Renounce immediately all sin(s) that He brings to mind (1 John 1:9).

III. We must have an intense desire for the fullness of the Holy Spirit in our lives (Matthew 5:6). We must come to the end of ourselves seeing all of our abilities as being inadequate.

A young minister, fresh out of Bible school, observed an elder minister preach obviously under the power of the Holy Spirit. The young man went to the elder and begged to be shown how to have such power in his preaching. The elder invited the young man to go fishing with him at a local pier later that day. The young man accepted the invitation, found the elder and sat down beside him. There were the customary greetings followed by silence for a long time. The young man, growing ever anxious to know the secret to the power of the Holy Spirit, asked when would he be told? At that point, the elder pushed the young man into the lake and held his head underwater. The young man was thrashing to surface and take a breath but the old man – stronger than he appeared, continued to hold the young man underwater. Just when the young man thought he would die, the elder pulled him out of the water. The young man took several deep breaths, and when partially recovered, asked the elder what was he trying to do? The elder replied that he was answering his question on how to have the power of God in your life. The young man said that he did not understand. The elder then stated that when he wanted the Holy Spirit upon him just like he wanted a breath of air – then he would have Him!

IV. We must ask (1) God the Father in Jesus' name for the Holy Spirit (Luke 11:13)

V. We must pray in faith (1) to receive the Holy Spirit (Matthew 21:22. Mark 11:24).

Heavenly Father, I confess the sin of trying to live the Christian life in my ability and power. I was ignorant of what was available to me in the new birth. I am laying down my life now for the ministry of Jesus Christ through me your servant. Please cause the Holy Spirit who lives within me to come/fall upon me that I might be anointed to continue the works of Jesus. Thank you. In Jesus Name, Amen.

Some of you will notice the change immediately. Others, God will have to align your will with His through trials so that the desire will be from your spiritual heart and not just your head. Nevertheless, if you have asked in faith, He will come upon you.

What if you have already received the Holy Spirit upon you (or the anointing of the Holy Spirit) but seemed to have lost or misplaced Him?

Timothy had received the Baptism of the Holy Spirit (Acts 16:1) and later the Anointing of the Holy Spirit (2 Timothy 1:6). Timothy was allowing the persecution that was coming against Christians, empowered by the spirit of fear (2 Timothy 1:7), to neutralize the Anointing of the Holy Spirit (2 Timothy 1:8). His heart had grown hard from timidity, timidity is a sin (Romans 14:23). Paul told him to start believing God and stepping out in faith to preach the Gospel and fellowship with those being persecuted to release the Anointing of the Holy Spirit, again (1 Timothy 4:11-16. John 7:37-39). We need to do like the early church in Jerusalem did when threatened – they prayed for more boldness! (Acts 4:24-33) Boldness is a result of the anointing!

CONCLUSION:

<u>There is a war between God's people and Satan's demons:</u>

Evil spirits and the Holy Spirit have always been present on the earth. In fact, Jesus refers to both of them at one point in His ministry when He says in:

Matthew 12:28 28 **NIV** 'But if it is by the Spirit of God that I drive out demons, then the kingdom of God has come upon you'.

There is a war between God's people and Satan's demons. The evil spirits will eventually lose when Jesus Christ returns someday. We live in an evil world, and it is only the Holy Spirit who can protect us. If you are not a Christian, you can discover why Jesus died for you. He did this for you and me. Jesus said, in Hebrews 10:7-10). 'Here I am - it is written about me in the scroll - I have come to do your will, O God." First, he said, "Sacrifices and offerings, burnt offerings and sin offerings you did not desire, nor were you pleased with them" (although the law required them to be made). Then he said, "Here I am, I have come to do your will." He sets aside the first to establish the second. And by that will, we have been made holy through the sacrifice of the body of Jesus Christ once for all. For you have been called for this purpose, since Christ also suffered for you, leaving you an example for you to follow in His steps, who committed no sin, nor was any deceit found in His mouth; and while being reviled, He did not revile in return; while suffering He uttered no threats, but kept entrusting Himself to him who judges righteously; and He Himself bore our sins in His body on the cross, that we might die to sin and live to righteousness; for by His wounds you were healed. For you were continually straying like sheep, but now you have returned to the Shepherd and Guardian of your souls. Jesus Christ Died for Our Sins That We Might Die to Sin.

Today, please accept Jesus Christ as your Lord and Saviour so that He can be the Lord of your life for ever and ever. Amen.

<u>Jesus Christ is in the entire Bible:</u>

In Genesis He is The Breath of Life.

In Exodus He is The Pass over Lamb

In Leviticus He is our High Priest

In Numbers He is not a human being that He should change His mind

In Deuteronomy He is a Prophet like unto Moses

In Joshua He is The Captain of our Salvation

In Judges He is our Judge and Law Giver

In Ruth He is our Kingsman Redeemer

In 1st and 2nd Samuel He is our Trusted Prophet

In Kings and Chronicles, He is our reigning King

In Ezra and Nehemiah, He is The Rebuilder of the broken down walls of our human life

In Esther He is our Modekai

In Job He is our ever Living Redeemer

In Psalms He is our Shepherd

In Proverbs and Ecclesiastes, He is our Wisdom

In Song of Songs He is our Loving Bridegroom

In Isaiah He is our Prince of Peace

In Jeremiah He is The Righteous Branch

In Lamentations He is The Weeping Prophet

In Ezekiel He is the wonderful four faced man

In Daniel He is the fourth man in the fiery furnace

In Hosea He is The Faithful Husband forever married to the back sliders

In Joel He is The Baptiser of The Holy Ghost and Fire

In Amos He is our Burden Bearer

In Obadiah He is The Mighty to save

In Jonah He is our Great Foreigner Missionary

In Micah He is The Messenger of the beautiful feet

In Nahum He is our Strength and Shield

In Habakkuk He is God's Evangelist

In Zephaniah He is Jesus our Saviour

In Haggai He is The Restorer of God's lost Heritage

In Zechariah He is the fountain opened up in the house of David for sin and uncleanness

In Malachi He is The son of righteousness rising with healing in His wings.

<u>Here is Jesus in the New Testament:</u>

In Matthew Jesus Christ is The King of the Jews.

In Mark Jesus is The Servant

In Luke Jesus is The Son of Man, feeling what we feel

In John Jesus is The Son of God

In Acts Jesus is The Saviour of The Word

In Romans Jesus is The Righteousness of God

In 1st Corinthians Jesus is The Rock that followed Israel

In 2nd Corinthians Jesus is The Triumphant -one, giving victory

In Galatians Jesus is your Liberty, He sets you free.

In Ephesians Jesus is The Head of The Church

In Philippians Jesus is The Head of your Joy

In Colossians Jesus is Your Completeness

In 1st and 2nd Thessalonians Jesus is Your Hope

In 1st Timothy Jesus is Your Faith

In 2nd Timothy Jesus is Your Stability

In Titus Jesus is Truth

In Philemon Jesus is Your Benefactor

In Hebrews Jesus is Your Profession

In James Jesus is The Foundation of Your Faith

In 1st Peter Jesus is your Example

In 2nd Peter Jesus is your Purity

In 1 John Jesus is Your Life

In 2 John Jesus is your Pattern

In John 3 Jesus is your Motivation

In Jude Jesus is The Foundation of Your Faith

In Revelation Jesus is Your coming King

Jesus is The First and The Last. The beginning and The End

He is The Keeper of all creation and the creator of all

He is The Architect of the Universe

And The Manager of all times

He always was, He always is and He always will be

Unmoved, unchanged, undefeated and never undone

He was bruised and brought healing!

He was pierced and eases pain!

He was dead and brought life!

He was persecuted and brought freedom!

He is risen and brings power!

He reigns and brings Peace

The world can't understand Him

The armies can't defeat Him

The schools can't explain Him and the leaders can't ignore Him

Herod couldn't kill Him and the Pharisees couldn't confuse Him

Nero couldn't crush Him

Hitler couldn't silence Him

The new age can't replace Him, He is alive, love, longevity and more

His goodness, kindness and Gentleness and God, He is Holy

Righteousness, Mighty, Powerful and pure

His ways are right and His word is eternal

His will is unchanging, and His mind is on me

He is my Redeemer, He is my Saviour, He is my God

He is my Peace. He is my Joy, He is my Comfort

He is my Lord and He rules my life.

ACKNOWLEDGMENTS

To my Mother Anna-Kerina Mudisi, who went to be with the Lord on the 11th October 2012, thank you for the incorruptible seed that you planted in my life from when I was very young. Rest in peace, you will always be in my heart for you will always be my Mum.

To my Father Alois P. Mudisi now in Canada, you have always been my inspiration, my role model, I love you so much, thank you for praying for me always.

To my God given husband Rev. Dr. Eric, thank you for your wonderful support. On every venture I am inspired to take, you always journey with me. I thank God for your life, I love you dearly.

To my dearest children: Felix, Flint, Fulton, Stanley, Storm and Sapphire, thank you for your patience and tolerance as you journeyed with me through the highs and lows of life, I couldn't have chosen better children if I had been given the choice, I love you all very much. May the Lord be your strong Tower may he build a hedge of protection around you. I know God has good plans for you, His thoughts will give you peace not of evil and to give you a future and a hope, when you call upon Him and pray to Him, He will listen. Hold fast to His promises and never give up in life. When you fail use that experience as a stepping stone and keep trying!

To my two Brothers; Fabian and Paul in Botswana and my sister, Bridget Ndhlovu in Canada, my sister in the UK Orla Edwards and two sisters in America, Tendai Mudisi Soley and Gertrude Mudisi and their families, thank you all for being there for me laughing with me allowing me to be me. May God continue to use you in His Kingdom, may He open door for you that no man can shut.

Last, but not least, my Brothers and Sisters in Christ, my prayer partners thank you for coming together in prayer, exhortation, and stirring up love and good works.

To my husband Rev. Dr. Eric and my children Sapphire and Stanley thank you for editing and proof reading my book, you are truly special, I love you all.

AUTHOR'S PROFILE

Name: Rev. Dr. Marcelline B. Mudisi – Robinson PhD(H)

Practising Christian- A Believer in Jesus Christ The Son of God.

Birthday: May 31st

Marital status: Married with six children aged between 19 and 39

Husband's name: Pastor Eric Robinson

Home Country: Zimbabwe

Founder of GAE College in Gaborone Botswana

Education: Studied CIMA at University of West England

Diploma in Christian Ministry (CRC London)

Own Business: Company Director – Formation and accounts etc. for new companies.

Ordained (together with my husband) in June 2014

Church: Jesus Kingdom Ministry

Church Duties: Joint Minister with my husband

Coordinator & Lecturer of Christ the Redeemer Bible College – Bristol Campus with my husband

Author of eight Books: Freedom, Restoration, Privileges, Transformation, Treasures. Saviour, The Blood of Jesus, 'His Image' and Power of The Holy Spirit.

Preacher of the word.

Current studies: Actively studying/ working towards Bachelor of Arts in Theology and Practical Christian Ministry through Roehampton University in London. U.K

NOTES

NOTES

-------- NOTES ------

ABOUT THE BOOK

The dramatic shift related to God's Holy Spirit that occurred on the Day of Pentecost, immediately following Christ's death and ascension to heaven. God's actions on that day were a monumental event in human history and in His great master plan of salvation. God's Holy Spirit was poured out and made available, not just to the disciples and Israel, but to nations far off and to all that God may call. Through His Spirit, God works for us and through us to bring us into His Kingdom.

1 Corinthians 12:7 NIV:
Now to each one the manifestation of the Spirit is given for the common good.

Jesus said in John 14:12 NIV, : Very truly I tell you, whoever believes in me will do the works, I have been doing, and they will do even greater things than these, because I am going to the Father.

Printed in the United States
By Bookmasters